The social lives of young children

The social lives of young children

Play, conflict and moral learning in day-care groups

Elly Singer
Dorian de Haan

With contributions from Anke van Keulen and Nienke Bekkema

uitgeverij
SWP

With the support of the Bernard van Leer Foundation.

The social lives of young children
Play, conflict and moral learning in day-care groups
Elly Singer
Dorian de Haan

ISBN 978 90 6665 857 8
NUR 854

Translated by Murray Pearson from the Dutch, original title: *Kijken, kijken, kijken.*
Over samenspelen, botsen en verzoenen bij jonge kinderen (ISBN 978 90 6665 709 0)

Foreword

This book is based on ten years of observational research in play-groups and day-care centres. This was pioneering work at first, small-scale investigations into the daily lives and language use of two- and three-year-olds, carried out by Utrecht and Amsterdam university students of developmental psychology and pedagogy, under the supervision of the authors of this book. When we began, there had been little research aimed at understanding and articulating the experience of young children with each other and with their teachers. Over the course of time we were able to make contact with a broad stream of international research designed to support pedagogical developments for young children in child care centres. This line of research is based on a constructivist theoretical approach that builds on the work of Piaget and of Vygotsky and on modern theories of the emotions such as those of Frijda and Fischer. We have collaborated with various institutes, including the Deutsche Jugend Institut (Kornelia Schneider), the University of Jyva¨skyla¨ in Finland (Maritta Hännikäinen) and the Victoria University of Wellington in New Zealand (Carmen Dalli). As a result of grants from the Bernard van Leer Foundation and the Dutch Children's Welfare Stamps Campaign, in late 2002 we were able to expand the scale of our research and to look at the way that children of different (Dutch, West Indian and Moroccan) ethnic backgrounds deal with clashes and squabbles during free play, and how their teachers supervise them when such conflicts arise. We were at last in a position to put aside the patchwork of small investigations and now develop our research plans systematically. We are very grateful to both these foundations for this chance! Although the choice of focusing on clashes was partly to meet a practical need - teachers have to meet the demands of quarrelling children - the pedagogical and research-related considerations were actually more important. A conflict is a moment during playing together when the relation is acutely challenged. As we shall demonstrate in this book, conflicts are not simply negative crises: they offer enormous potential for learning new skills and important social and moral rules.

Ninety six two- and three-year-olds took part in this research, evenly divided between the two age groups, between boys and girls and between the three ethnic groups. All the children were in multi-ethnic groups, never with more than sixty percent of native Dutch children. In total, children were observed in free play in 23 childcare centres, using video and audio-recordings. Their mothers were also interviewed over the way they dealt with conflicts between young children at home: for the most part these were mothers of the children taking part in the investigation. Unless otherwise stated, all numerical data in this book are based on our own research. Most of the photos have been taken from the video-material. This has the disadvantage that these images are less sharp than ordinary photographs; but they have the advantage that they allow us, by selecting frames from the video-material, to demonstrate moments from an account or course of events. Thanks to an additional grant from the Bernard van Leer Foundation we have been able to illustrate this book with these photographs in colour.

The book is intended for a broad public; indeed, for all those who have an interest in what transpires between young children together in childcare centres, and in particular for teachers. We have translated our scientific findings and those of others into practical terms, since in the end practise is what it is all about. Teachers are the key to good quality child day-care. It depends largely on them whether children have a good time with each other and whether they can learn and play well together. Over the past ten years we have regularly published reports of our research in scientific journals. Articles on our most recent work are in preparation. The list of references at the back of this book will direct you to specific aspects of our scientific work and also to the wider field of international research to which our work belongs.

Without the contributions of a great many people this book could never have been realized. In the first place, Anke van Keulen, author of chapters 13, 36 and 37, has been involved with our research from the very beginning and has especially given us deeper insight into inter-cultural communication and the way that diversity is handled in child day-care centres. Since 1989, from the Bureau MUTANT she has carried out development work in the field of diversity and particularly in special training for teachers and managers working with parents and children of different ethnic backgrounds. In addition to her written contribution, she also gave constructive commentary on our early drafts of the book. We are particularly pleased that she has developed a training programme for teachers based on our research. In the second place we would like to mention Nienke Bekkema, the junior researcher who assembled and analysed much of the data, and has made an important scientific contribution to our research. She was responsible for the selection - especially for this book - of one hundred and sixty photos from the video-material. Anke and Nienke were our main supports: we were able to share with them our pleasure in the observation of the children, and for this we owe them a great 'thank you'!

Beside these two stalwarts there are others we would like to thank who have made important contributions to the text. Aafke Huisman helped write the chapters on babies and made photographs available to us. Without her knowledge and enthusiasm those chapters could not have been written. Ana del Barrio Saiz, Didy van Brandwijk, Eeke de Graaf, Anja Hol, Loes Kleerekoper, Trees Pels, Wilma Poot and Liesbeth Schreuder provided generous commentary on our several drafts, the result of which has been a huge improvement in the clarity of the book. We are very grateful for the insights they have so willingly shared with us, but they should not be held accountable for any contentious views that remain in our book: we alone are responsible for the final text.

The technical assistance of Frank Hamers was a great support during the filming in child day-care centres. He helped us find solutions to the problems of combining sound and image. The following students have also made significant contributions: in alphabetical order in the context of their Masters degree in Pedagogy or Developmental Psychology, Odile Agterberg, Fatiha Ben Messaoud, Marte Bolk, Liliana Booy, Mirjam-Moniek Elskamp, Liza Fransisco, Maggie Gernaat, Ellen van de Glind, Hadassa Heidsieck, Anne-Greth van Hoogdalem, Leontien Korteweg, Lonneke de Kraker, Patricia Kruitbosch, Jojanneke van de Kuilen, Fredelief van der Mast, Danielle Min, Judith van Nes, Hester van Ooijen, Leonie Ouwerkerk, Saskia Pinkers, Dorien van Ree, Fleur de Sain, Saskia Saunier, Rachel Semeijn, Noortje Terwindt, Patricia Vermeulen, Saaske Verstraete, Astrid de Vries en Lisbeth Wijngaarden. Thank you all! Amina Rourou deserves a special mention; she was our second junior researcher and was in particular responsible for interviewing mothers. Chapter 36 is based on her work. This part of our research goes beyond the scope of this book; we shall publish more extensively on it elsewhere. Amina enriched our team meetings with her knowledge of Moroccan culture and changes within it in the Dutch context.
And, of course, at least as important as subsidies and help with the research and the writing of the book is the cooperation of the children, their parents, the teachers and the institutions where we have been able to conduct our research. We have always been given a warm welcome and were always able to return with our audio- and video-apparatus and questions, sometimes several weeks later. We hope that with this book we can repay something of what we have been able to learn, thanks to your cooperation!

Elly Singer
Dorian de Haan

Contents

Introduction

Looking, listening, talking together and thinking, that is what bringing up young children is all about. But looking at what? All four of us - Dorian, Anke, Nienke en Elly – have had experience of enthusiastic colleagues who observed interesting forms of cooperation on video where we ourselves saw nothing there but a bunch of swarming children. You have to learn to observe! And that is the principle aim of this book. Over the past ten years we have investigated the way two- and three-year-old children play together: how they play together and how they make clear what they want, how they joke, how they clash with each other and how they make up again – and, moreover, how teachers can help children. Slowly but surely we discovered patterns.

The book is essentially about playing together, getting into conflicts and making up afterwards among young children in playgroups and day-care centres. We have devoted a great deal of attention to the way a feeling of togetherness, of contact and mutual understanding, arises between a teacher and a child, and also between two children. Our starting assumption is that a good relationship is the basis of everything: of the sense of security, of being connected and of being someone with his or her own identity; of the desire to get to know each other and to learn together; and of the motivation to make peace again after a clash.

It has become a book with many short chapters, thematically ordered, each of which can be read separately from the others. First of all, there is the basis of everything: the making contact and the experience of being together (Part 1). We then look at the way new children and parents find a place for themselves in the group and get to feel at home (Part 2). We look in detail at conflicts between children and their reconciliation (Parts 3 and 4), and the unwritten social rules and skills that they develop together. Young children actually seem to be very good at resolving problems when these crop up between them – certainly no worse than the teachers or other adults – though this does not mean that teachers don't have an important role in the communal life and play of children (Part 5). Special attention is given to the way differences and diversity are handled: younger and older children, difficult children and differences of sex and ethnicity (Part 6).

Being a teacher is an occupation that demands great personal involvement and creativity; it is an occupation to be proud of!

Democracy

Bringing up children requires more than observing and listening to them, it's also a matter of values and norms that you want to convey to them. In Dutch society, these are democratic values and norms. This may sound rather portentous in the context of thinking about two- and three-year-old children, yet the same social questions arise when children are together as disturb the lives of adults. This is how children learn the social skills and rules that form the basis of our society; learn to share, to care for each other and to respect the uniqueness of each individual. The latter means that there is also respect for the parents, the family and the social and cultural background of the children. In this book we show how, together with the parents, teachers in child care centres can help young children to develop democratic values, and skills.

The miracle

Children can do much that adults do, but they do it in their own way. For example, they can react just as strongly to injustice, but their approach is different. If they have hurt someone, the feeling of guilt is clearly visible on their faces. Their passions can flare openly when a parent or teacher does something they find very unfair. They have an acute sense of limits and boundaries. Whoever has witnessed that peculiar little laugh of a child who knows he or she has done something naughty will never forget it.

In fact, young children can do some things much better than adults. They are much more forgiving, their quarrels are over much more quickly and they are cleverer - in fact, their rate of learning is many times that of adults. The miracle is how they look at the unfamiliar and discover what they don't yet know in the process of doing it.

Security and belonging

Even so, we should not overestimate young children. They need their parents and trusted teachers. If they are uncertain they look questioningly toward the adults who happen to be at hand, trusting that they will look after them. This is why personal contact is so important, contact where children feel themselves known. This is what gives them the secure base from which they can go out into the world. Teachers have also to ensure that children feel safe and confident among themselves, that children will not hurt each other and will not irritate each other. A good child care centre is characterised by positive relations between the children and a happy 'we-feeling'.

The wrong attention

The vulnerability of young children evokes in adults a reaction to take care of them. This is fine, but they can also miss the point entirely. Parents and teachers sometimes involve themselves in things without understanding exactly what is going on. They often don't know what a child wants or feels and cannot then simply put things right for the child. When they pick out a guilty party in a quarrel, they often get it wrong because they haven't seen what happened before. Moreover, they deprive children of the room to learn through discovery and to find solutions themselves.

Doing it together

Young children learn and think through doing. Parents and teachers need to be aware of this when they want to teach them something. Directions must be as concrete as possible: no long stories and no abstract language; not 'Be quiet' but 'Go and sit nice and comfy on your mattress with a book.' Playing with them and showing them how to do something also offer golden opportunities to learn together through doing.

Talking, talking, talking

Talking involves more than just words. In fact, children can talk very well without words. By imitating somebody a child can make it clear that he or she understands the other. The fact that a child cannot yet talk much does not mean that the adult also has to remain silent. On the contrary, children learn most from the teacher when they do things together and the teacher gives a running commentary on what's happening. In addition, it is important to give children a voice, even the very youngest. Ask children what they want and when they run into problems ask them whether they have a plan. Despite their limited command of words young children are very good partners for thinking together.

Developing one's creativity

This book is full of observations, research findings and interpretations of children's and teachers' behaviour. We also offer tips to all involved in educating young children. Our aim is to invite you to look, listen, to talk and think together with them. Perhaps you will come to different or new findings. No one ever finishes learning, and in this regard children and adults are alike. Everything you learn, each person has to discover afresh.

The aim of this book

This book is intended for all involved in the upbringing of young children: teachers in play-groups and day-care centres and parents. It is also intended to be used by students. The book teaches you how to look better at children and provides insights into group events and into the behaviour of teachers. You will find suggestions for further thought, pedagogical practise and references to other literature and training schemes.

Associated with this book, the training programme* 'You can learn from clashes' comes in two forms: one for teachers and one for supervisors/instructors. The following questions are at the heart of the programme: what can teachers and carers do to create mutual involvement and communal play among children in the group? How do they deal with clashes between children? When should they and when should they not intervene? How can they help children to learn basic social values, rules and skills through play?

---

* You can learn from clashes. Workshops and training for teachers on how to deal with clashes between teachers and parents.

I am me and you are you. Dealing with diversity. Training-the-trainers course for teachers and trainers on how to deal with diversity with young children, parents and your colleagues.

From Bureau MUTANT. Information: www.mutant.nl and a.vankeulen@mutant.nl

Part 1

TOGETHER

1   'Together' is the basic principle

Very young children are dependent on others and react directly to what they feel and to what others do with them. A safe and trusting relationship is the basis for everything with them. If they feel safe and at home, they dare to open up, to make contact, experiment, joke and even risk getting into a quarrel - because everything works out in the end if you trust each other.

Adults also sense when they can trust someone; but what is it exactly that they pick up on? This is not such an easy question to answer: one's sense of security is usually self-evident. One way of getting some idea of what happens is to call to mind somebody with whom you feel very much at ease, then ask yourself the following question: When exactly do I most strongly feel secure and happy with this person? If it's a matter of fathers and mothers, the answers will refer to memories such as: 'they were always there when I needed them'; 'that feeling of companionship with my father in the car, driving somewhere to he had to go before his work'; 'laughing together, singing and playing games' or 'listening to the stories my mother used to tell'. It always comes back to situations where people do things together in which they feel good together.

The same is true for young children: they feel sure of themselves when others understand their needs. It feels good when the other person is on your wavelength, when it clicks with the other person. So the basis of trust lies in the way we deal with each other concretely, in what we do. This principle holds for everybody, but especially for young children. This is why we begin our book with chapters on how teachers and children in childcare centres create that sense of togetherness: through physical contact, through eye contact, gestures, taking turns, by imitating and inviting children to imitate, through joking and playing games that are predictable but nonetheless exciting, playing together with words and communal games with words. Reciprocity is an absolutely key concept.

2 First experiences of being together

What babies feel and think, we just don't know. They can't tell us and as adults we can no longer remember how it was. But simply by observing closely we can see very well when a baby is relaxed or feels happy. The realisation of being together is something you evoke from each other and give shape to together. Babies make an active contribution, as do teachers. Together they create a shared reality.

Working together with the baby

Miriam, the teacher, walks toward the four-month-old Anna, who lies on the ground playing with her fingers. Miriam waits till she looks away from her fingers and says: 'Hi , Anna, are you lying comfortably?' She waits until Anna is looking at her and makes a movement with her mouth. 'I'm going to take you and clean you.' Miriam again waits until Anna makes a noise and then holds out her hands. She picks Anna up and finds the right way to hold her so that she lies comfortably in her arms. Rocking her gently, she walks with Anna to the dressing table. 'So, I'm going to put you on the dressing table. Are you comfortable? Shall I take your pants off?' She touches her leg and waits for Anna to start moving her leg herself, then lifts her bottom up and pulls her pants off. 'Now your top.' The nappy has to be changed. 'Look, I'm putting the dirty nappy in the bath.' Anna looks with interest at what Miriam is doing. There is eye contact. 'So, now I'm going to wipe your bottom clean: here's the flannel, see it?' Miriam waits until she sees that Anna is looking at the flannel. 'This feels a bit cold, doesn't it!' Miriam watches Anna while she does this and

Talking together, showing the nappy

Looking outside together

19

imitates her facial expression. Anna looks intently at Miriam. 'Now, see, here is the clean nappy!' And so on: this is how they collaborate in the changing of nappies. After each action Miriam waits to give Anna the time to react.

You feel it, you see it

The experience of togetherness and being understood is an active process to which both partners contribute. Together they create an inter-subjective reality (Stern, 2002). But with babies, this inter-subjectivity and the sense of togetherness mainly arise through non-verbal communication (Doherty-Sneddon, 2003). The most important ways of communicating non-verbally are:
- *Body contact*, touching each other. Miriam holds Anna comfortably in her arms and rocks her gently. She gives Anna the experience of having passive body contact.
- *Gestures*. Miriam holds out her hands in a gesture of invitation. She makes skin contact with her hand and waits for a reaction from Anna.
- *Eye contact*. As soon as Anna looks at Miriam, she picks her up. They read each other's faces.
- *Facial expression and imitation*. Anna moves her mouth and Miriam copies her. Miriam imitates Anna's behaviour and in her imitation she shows clearly that she is pleased with Anna's reactions.
- *Talking with babies* is also very important. Teachers accompany their actions with language. They always say what they are going to do, they say what they think the baby sees or wants and what they are doing. Miriam's voice and Anna's reaction to it: these too are a significant part of the way togetherness is created.

Pedagogical tips to remember

- Collaborative work between teachers and babies from six weeks old begins with making eye contact with the baby.

- The teacher tells the baby what she is doing and what she is going to do. If the baby is distracted, she talks about what has caught the baby's attention.

- This collaborative work is a question of always taking turns in doing things.

- As teacher, you should always pay attention to the baby's own tempo! Make sure to follow an action on the part of the baby with an imitation or reaction.

- After an action, the teacher waits for a reaction from the child.

3 Play-talk between baby and teacher

'Play-talking' between baby and teacher begins from the age of four months. The teacher combines all the baby's movements and sounds into a game. From seven or eight months onward, babies themselves increasingly take more initiative (Ninio & Snow, 1996). Baby and teacher have intense eye contact, take turns in making noises, exchanging gestures and grimaces, both greatly enjoying the fun. They imitate, play, converse and challenge each other.

Peekaboo

Daan (0;10) sits on the dressing table and laughs at Inge, the teacher. Inge laughs back. Daan has a cloth in his hand and pulls it over his head. He waits a while and then suddenly pulls it off again. He regards Inge, full of expectation and with a roguish look on his face. Wide-eyed, she looks back at him with feigned astonishment. Daan shouts with laughter and immediately repeats the operation. On his initiative, they go on playing this game with increasing enthusiasm. Daan puts the cloth ever more wildly over his head and Inge pretends ever more amazement and with louder exclamations: 'What! Is it you again!' Dan tries to put the cloth over Inge's face. This is only half successful, but from the pleasure in their eyes you can see that the intention has been understood by both and that the pleasure is no less. Dan then allows himself to be brought to bed, the cloth still over his head.

Peeka?

boo!

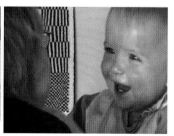
Haha!

Familar patterns of action

Simple face-to-face interactions are a source of pleasure for both baby and teacher (Schaffer, 1977). With children younger than six months, this interactive game is mainly initiated by the teacher, who always waits for the baby's action and then imitates it, making the same noises or pulling the same face. After making the same noise, she can continue with a brief sentence such as in the following sequence:

Baby: 'Huh.'

Teacher: 'yes, that's nasty, filthy thing.' This mimicking of the child can be exaggerated, with the expression of an emotion being stressed. In this way children may find it easier to learn to recognise emotions.

A slightly older baby will itself start to imitate the teacher. When the teacher looks somewhere, the child will follow her gaze. Games in which baby and teacher challenge and surprise each other then begin, such as peekaboo, and as a result of repetition, familiar patterns of action and rituals develop. Doing and saying things by turns are now well established – what linguists refer to as 'proto-conversation'; the interchange of the baby's babbling and the comments and questions of the teacher make it seem like a real conversation.

Emergence of self-awareness and moral awareness

Out of the familiar patterns of action and the feeling of we-together arises the awareness of having a will of one's own. That is, the child gradually becomes aware that it can influence others. For example, the baby discovers that laughing enhances the chances that the teacher will stay and continue with play-talking. The baby also discovers that if it imitates the teacher and looks wherever she looks, new and exciting things can happen. Without a predictable environment and familiar patterns of action with teachers a baby is powerless, except when it starts crying. But this latter is a negative attention, out of necessity. According to some psychologists, the capacity to do things by turns (reciprocity) is not only the basis of communication but also of moral awareness (Van Emde, Biringer, Clyman & Oppenheim, 1991). The great pleasure that comes from doing something by turns is a strong motive to please others. The principle of 'don't do to others what you would not want to happen to yourself' is based on reciprocity and its seed lies in early infancy. Crowing with pleasure, evoking togetherness and the first awareness of a 'self' (that you yourself can bring something about) and involvement with the other: these are all part and parcel of the same development.

Pedagogical tips to remember

Reciprocal interactions give the feeling of contact and of being understood.

Reciprocity can be promoted in several ways:

- by doing the same as the other: mirroring or imitating;
- by reacting as the other expects in the usual routines, customs, games and rituals, or by saying beforehand what you are going to do;
- by surprising the other and making sure that the other is pleasantly surprised and not frightened.

4 Personal and cultural differences in creating togetherness

By no means all adults play-talk with babies. There are different preferences in the matter. Furthermore, different cultures have different ways of evoking togetherness and different rules about the right distance, the proper degree of closeness. There are contact cultures and cuddling teachers, and there are more distant teachers and cultures. (Doherty-Sneddon, 2003).

Getting cuddles from the teacher

The teacher, Siglin, sits at a table with several children who are doing puzzles. Megan (2;9) approaches and nestles up close to Siglin, who lifts her up, sets her on her lap and says: 'Hi, Megan, look, they're doing puzzles.' Megan shows little interest, but rather abandons herself to Siglin's cuddles and kisses while, all the time, Siglin goes on quietly talking to the other children. After a few minutes, Megan has had her fill and slips off Siglin's lap to go in the direction of another group of children, in search of some new activity.

Reading aloud, with all the children lying on a mattress

Ingrid the teacher sits on the mattress – with cushions supporting her back – and reads aloud from a book with rather splendid pictures. Five children are lying half against her and half against each other. They are clearly enjoying the physical contact, Ingrid's voice, the story and the togetherness.

Cuddling

A kiss

In our research we found major differences in the degree of physical contact between teachers and children. Some teachers are generous and frequent cuddlers, while others cuddle rarely. Culture, personal preference and customs within different day-care centres all play a role in determining these differences.

Cultural differences

Somewhere in the middle of Peru, I (Elly) spent several hours with Indian women and babies waiting for a bus that never actually arrived. Without thinking, I began to talk with the babies, imitating their noises and pulling faces, all to the great amazement of the mothers. These western women are crazy! I later realised that these mothers and babies mainly experience their togetherness through physical contact, not facial expressions. The baby is carried on the mother's back and at the market sleeps contentedly against her mother while she is busy with her customers. There is constant physical proximity. The two bodies are attached to each other and a small baby can happily pass hours like this without demanding much attention. This seemed to me fine for the children, restful and calm: they don't have to do anything in order to be with their mother. If an Indian baby and mother wanted to indulge in play-talk like Western babies and mothers, the mother would scarcely be able to take her child to work with her. People from Southern Europe, the Arabic culture and South America complain that West- and North-Europeans and North Americans are cold and distant. The West Indian and Moroccan mothers I interviewed also often found the Dutch too lacking in warmth and involvement. Contact cultures are more tolerant of physical proximity: people more readily stare at other people and touch each other more. The Westerners expect more physical distance and find staring ill-mannered, while touching is limited to handshakes and short, friendly eye contact. Westerners mainly make contact with each other through eyes and speech.

Reading aloud

Talk-teacher

Differences between children and adults

The younger the child, the more physical contact is allowed. In all cultures, there are special rules for young children. Babies and toddlers are allowed to nestle up to anybody, to walk into them or pull their hair without the other getting angry. Babies even crawl over each other without protest from the other baby. Even most dogs accept it when a toddler pulls their tail. If it hurts, they try to walk away, but dogs seldom bite - a tolerance that is probably biologically determined. Because young children are much less threatening than older children or adults, infringing personal space is not so readily interpreted as a threat or a signal of dominance. On the other hand, any strange adult who picks up or wants to kiss a baby or toddler is an enormous threat to the child!

Personal differences

Cuddle-babies love to lie against you and be cuddled. Other children have little 'talent' for being a baby. They tense their bodies when you pick them up and seem to be more at ease when they can crawl. These babies find togetherness with their parents or teacher easier to achieve by means of romping games and play-talk. There are children with an easier temperament who more easily make contact with adults, and children with a more difficult temperament, who maintain their distance or react to contact quite vehemently. Adults also differ in their needs of contact. There are cuddling teachers, doing-things-together teachers and eye-and-talk-contact teachers. This is not entirely dissimilar to what one sees between different partners after a row. One will restore unity by talking, another only feels fully together again by cuddling and yet another by making love.

Pedagogical tips to remember

If, as a teacher, you find that it's difficult to make contact with a child or to comfort or calm a child, then two things are important:

1. Ask the parents how they make contact with their child; how they handle the baby during cleaning, playing, comforting and calming. Perhaps there are cultural differences or family habits that are too different from the way you are used to behaving with children. Ask their advice and look for solutions together.

2. Talk with your colleagues and together look for new approaches. For each child there is a key! Difficult temperaments don't exist: there are only combinations of children and teachers or parents that are less suited to each other.

5 Babies and toddlers among themselves

From a very early age, babies show an interest in each other. As soon as they can move their head they are drawn to other children. They try to touch each other and are very tolerant with regard to each other. Whereas babies become anxious with adult strangers, they are hardly ever afraid of strange babies. Teachers and peers have a very different role in children's lives.

Playing together at the baby's level

Jason (0;9) sits on the rug on the ground holding a rattle. He strikes the ground with his arm so that the rattle makes a noise. Margy's (0;10) attention is attracted by this noise and she crawls toward Jason. When Jason stops, she reaches toward the rattle, but Jason pulls his arm back and begins to rattle again. Margy watches. By chance she finds a plastic ball with something inside it. When Jason stops again, she begins to rattle with the ball. Jason now looks attentively at Margy and when she stops he recommences his own rattling. They look at each other and laugh.

Making contact

Merel (0;5) holds an interesting toy in her hand, but her attention is mainly directed toward Bram (0;5). She touches his arm and laughs at him, but Bram is looking more intently at Merel's toy and doesn't notice her attempt at contact. Merel persists and, still looking at him, tries to touch his hand and with her hand strokes his face. At this, Bram looks at her and Merel gets a beaming smile from him in return.

Seeking contact	Lucas crawls over Sarah	And back again

Looking questioningly at the teacher

As a rule, when babies are together they seek contact with the teacher by looking at her. Lauri (0;11) sits on the rug with her doll next to her. Lidy (1;0) wants to take the doll, but immediately Lauri grasps the doll tightly. With big eyes and a bit tense, she looks in the direction of the teacher. (Is this allowed? Will you help me?).

Imitation play

Babies get so much experience with each other that even as toddlers they are well able to judge the other child's mood. They already have the feeling for being silly with each other and can even accept it if the other one wants to do something different in their playing together. Judy Dunn (1988, pp. 111, 113) describes how imitation play demonstrates that toddlers of eighteen months are already capable of sensing and understanding the mood and actions of the other. They also understand what another wants in his play and how they can join in with their play.

Homour

With a brmmmm noise, a three-year-old boy races with his toy bicycle toward a young toddler (1;6). The toddler laughs and runs away. He imitates the older boy by grabbing a block and rushing toward him making the same kind of noise. Laughing and screaming, the two of them then race with their 'racing bikes' through the room. The boy falls and, still laughing, the young toddler imitates him, gives him a hand and pulls him up. This is later repeated with, this time, the toddler falling and being pulled up again by the older boy. Later in the afternoon the boy plays out a story with dolls. The toddler stands by watching and laughs. He then goes to the cupboard, chooses dolls that are suitable for the game and gives them to the child.

| Merel wants Maria's book | Maria hits Merel | Maria and Merel - nothing wrong |

Up to the late seventies, child psychologists assumed that children younger then four were not really capable of playing together (Singer, 2002; 2005). It was thought that babies had no interest in each other and could not yet do things together. Toddlers were supposed to be too egocentric and their contacts with other toddlers were mainly conflictive. However, since ever more young children have gone to day-care centres and psychologists have been able to investigate their life together it has become clear that young children too are very much involved with each other. Recent research has also revealed a rather different picture. Young children in childcare centres derive their basic safety from their relationship with teachers, it is true, but from a very young age they also have contact with each other.

Children are by their nature oriented toward communication (Schaffer, 1977) and begin communicating as soon as others stimulate them and respond. An adult who plays a game of give and take will usually make it easy for the baby by taking long pauses and expressly inviting the baby to take its turn. But another baby has its own ideas and can, for example, refuse, presenting the baby with a challenge to find a new solution to this conflict. Margy's behaviour described earlier is a good example of this. Adults commonly imitate a baby's facial expressions, gestures and noises; but a baby also imitates what others do - as in the example of Jason and Margy. The first forms of reciprocal imitation, eye contact and cooperation by taking turns in doing something, are developed during the period between six and twelve months. Babies use the social rules of reciprocity to understand each other. Playing with peers provides the child with the opportunity to penetrate the mental world of the other; not only the world of emotions, as when they laugh together, but also the world of thoughts: understanding what the other wants. These are a child's first steps toward an understanding of mind, i.e. understanding what others think, feel and desire.

Singing together

Choo-choo puff-puff

Isabel looks attentively at Onno

Rules of reciprocity

In relationships with parents and teachers, the child gains experience of the rules of reciprocity. These social and moral rules also form the basis of young children's relationships with each other. By playing with each other and through clashes the children learn with each other:
- To give and to receive.
- To take turns actively.
- Showing how and imitating.
- When someone is friendly toward you, you are friendly back.
- If you do something nasty to somebody, there is good chance they will be nasty to you.
- When you have done something wrong, make it good again.
- If someone else is smaller than you, or can do less, adapt yourself to them.

It is against the rules of reciprocity to make use of greater power or to get your own way just because you are stronger.

Pedagogical tips to remember

- The babies must above all feel confident and welcome with their teachers.

- Babies that are satisfied with the attention they get from the teacher relax and probably have easier contacts with other children.
  Both in contact with the teacher and with peers they gain experience of the rules of reciprocity.

6 Toddlers' associative play - 'part-together-part-alone'

For two- and three-year-olds, playing with and being among other children are some of the greatest attractions of the children's day-care centre. Toddlers try to get close to each other during free play. They play in parallel with each other, they run after each other, they play imitation games, then go off and do something on their own (Stambak & Sinclair, 1993; Verba,1994). They play 'part-together-part-alone'. Indeed, during free play, toddlers communicate more with each other than they do with the teacher.

Associative play: part-together-part-alone

Jan seems to have a definite idea, as he is all the time building on to a train. Raahi occasionally helps Jan, but if his gaze happens to fall somewhere else he will spend some time playing there. Sometimes he sits and sings and then starts playing again with a piece of plastic, his 'motorcar'. Waldy would like to help build the train with Jan, but that is not part of Jan's scheme. So Waldy plays now and again with him, then plays in parallel with duplo, close to where Jan is constructing his train, and then goes to play near Jordi, who is playing a little further away. Jordi is playing with duplex blocks and wheels without actually constructing anything. He helps Jan a few times and he accepts the fact that Waldy is giving his wheels to Jan for the train. Sometimes he joins in singing with Raahi. There are at least five different games going on near and across each other – sometimes alone, sometimes together, sometimes in parallel and imitative. Despite minor disagreements – particularly with Jan who seems to have very definite ideas – the whole scene seems peaceful and for a long time they play part-together-part-alone.

Together   On their own

Wholly absorbed in what she sees

33

Taking-it-in-gaze

Josey (3;4) accidentally falls over Jasper (3;5) who immediately begins to hit her. Sally (3;0) sits on the sofa watching in a concentrated fashion. A furious conflict develops between Josey and Jasper. Sally remains looking on and if anything happens outside her field of view she shifts on the sofa in order to be able to see better. To the end, Sally remains sitting and watching until, eventually, the teacher puts a stop the conflict.

Different kinds of play in free play

Various investigations have looked at what two to three-year-old children actually do during free play, how often they play on their own and how often they play with others. What this research seems to show is that there are huge differences depending on the age of the children involved and the way in which teachers support the communal play. Toddlers spend most of the time close to each other either playing together or in parallel, and for the rest they play on their own, keeping an eye on what the others are doing. The least time is spent communicating with the teacher (Schindler, Moely & Frank, 1987; Berk, 1997). This is shown in the diagram below, which is based on an estimate derived from both our own research and that of others in other countries. When children are a little older, there is an increase in both solitary play and playing together with communal goals or rules.

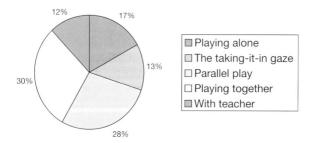

Playing alone
The taking-it-in gaze
Parallel play
Playing together
With teacher

Playing alone

Parallel play

We make a distinction between the following kinds of play:

- *Playing alone* – the child plays alone with its own body or with objects, or looks at a book.
- *The taking-it-in gaze* – the child gazes around wide-eyed and attentively, as though registering everything, trying to understand what's going on. Young children are not yet able to scan their surroundings and observe in the way that adults do. In order to register something they have to concentrate on that one thing at a time.
- *Parallel play* – children play close to each other with similar materials They appear not to communicate much with each other , but if one watches the video closely one sees that there are invariably moments of imitation, exchanges of objects or minor conflicts that arise because children have taken each other's objects or taken too much room. There is no fixed boundary between this and the following kind of play.
- *Part-together-part-alone play (associative play)* – communal play can simply develop between the children without premeditation, either by one child expressly inviting another to imitate what he is doing (e.g. looking at the other, doing something, looking at him again and so on until the other copies what he or she is doing) or by the other child spontaneously imitating (e.g. joining in the building of another child's tower). Sometimes the game can be running after each other, stopping and then running again. Children may also begin by offering some object, or with a verbal proposition, or they may play 'part-together-part-alone' because the play partners also follow their own ideas. Playing together and playing by oneself alternate. Different storylines or ideas can intersect. Perhaps this can best be compared with the way adults behave at a party with everybody talking, just walking away, laughing together, sometimes listening to each other and sometimes following their own associations.
- *Playing together with a communal goal, plan or rules* – this kind of play often develops in the third year. The articulation of plans here plays a greater role. For example, in pretend games the roles are divided ('You're the baby' and 'I'm the mother'). However, the degree of cooperation between children depends to a large extent on the environment and therefore on the teacher.

Having a blanket fight

Chasing away monsters together

Pedagogical tips to remember

- When two- and three-year-olds play together it often becomes a matter of playing-part-together-part-alone. You can very quickly tune into this by first watching one child and then another. It is an important insight if you want to help children with their play together.

- Pay close attention to children's taking-it-in gaze. This gives information on what holds their interest most and enables the teacher to adjust to this.

7 How children create a 'we-feeling'

Children love being together and they show it very plainly. They do this very early by gazing at each other intently, touching and imitating each other.

Ohhh! Ohhh! Imitation play

Jouri sticks his head between the cupboard and the wall and shouts 'Ohhh!' loudly. He comes back, looks at Emma, dives back again between the cupboard and the wall and again shouts 'Ohhh!'. Again, he looks straight at Emma. Emma has now understood. She bends toward the cupboard and wall and also shouts 'Ohhh!' , upon which Jouri once again bends between the cupboard and wall and calls 'Ohhh!', laughing. Emma again imitates his shout but gives the game a new twist. She turns in the direction of the wall and – shouting 'Ohhh!'– waves with her hands. Jouri immediately picks up on this and extends the game further. Going up to the cupboard he bumps his head against the wood. Emma imitates him. Jouri shouts enthusiastically: 'Do it again.'

Once language development is under way, children also discover linguistic ways of expressing togetherness (De Haan & Singer, 2001). Indeed, young children find being together so important they are often heard talking about it. They are very keen to let it be known that they're both there and that they both have the same things.

Looking at what Jouri is doing

Jouri is happy

Greeting

Thomas (4;0) (with emphasis): 'Hi, Cas, hi!'

Showing what they have together

Having the same things: 'I got peanut butter too!'

Being the same:

> Bob (2;10): 'I'm a monkey.'
> Cas (3;2): 'Me too, I'm a monkey too.'
> Bob: 'You a monkey too!'

Emphasising the 'we':

> Suzanne (3;4): 'So we going in the lift. We going in the lift. We going in the lift. Going in the lift.'

Nominating friendship

> Cas (3;5): 'you're my friend, aren't you?'
> Chantal (2;11): 'Yes'
> Cas: 'And Bob's my friend too.'
> Chantal: 'I am too, I am too, I'm Leanne's friend too'.

They also express this desire to belong with each other by demonstrating that they like the other.

Use of nicknames, abbreviations for the names of others

> 'No, don't clear up there, Silly-billy.'
> 'Em' or 'Emmie' for 'Emma.'

Looking and pointing together

Waving together

Imitation play is a more important way of celebrating being together. We have already seen this above when the two-year-old Jouri and Emma were copying each other, but language offers wonderful possibilities.

Imitation play with words

> Kasper: 'This puppy.'
> Cas: 'You you you're this puppy.
> Kasper: 'You' this poppy'
> Cas: 'No, you're this puppy. You're this puppy, this pup.'
> Kasper: 'This pup.'
> Cas: 'You are this pup, this, you're this pup.'
> Kasper: 'You are this pup.'
> Cas: 'And you're this poop!'

Intimate language

Just like adults, children are also found to use intimate language, language one uses to make clear what one feels for someone. But with young children this intimate language sometimes appears rather different from that of adults (De Haan & Singer, 2003). Young children are open in their expression of affection and aversion. Non-verbally they do this through touching if they're fond of somebody and crying loudly and turning away if they don't want anything to do with someone. Three-year-old children still have no bar against saying it when they like being together or be the other's friend. At the day-care centre they spend a lot of time gazing at each other, talking about the same thing and about being together. Repeating to each other is a kind of declaration of love: I am (at this moment) very keen on you.... At the after-school care centre, when they are a year older, this openness has already been somewhat reined in. Their alliances are then more evident in their communal play, which becomes more predominant at this age. Declaring friendships is something done in both periods, but as they grow older this is more often conditional: 'Shall we play football? Then I'll be your best friend!' The games of imitation and language play whereby children let it be known that they want to be with each other are now replaced by exclamations, such as: 'Wow, man!'

- Take time regularly to watch children and ask yourself: how do these children evoke the feeling of being together?

- If a child has difficulty making friends, try to find out what exactly that child is doing that repels other children, and also when contact does work successfully.

- Join in with the children's spontaneous way of evoking togetherness. Exploit, for example, their 'we-together' feeling by getting them to recite together ritual formulae, such as, "all having bread and jam" when they cannot do it themselves. Or you can teach them a song or verse with gestures that express the idea "we are friends". Play together with children, especially with children that tend to remain more by themselves and invite others to join you as well. By playing games, teach them to become adept at being-together.

8 How teachers help to create the 'we-feeling'

Teachers have a great influence on the quality of children's communal play. They do it by evoking a we-feeling with each child individually, i.e. the teacher one-on-one with each particular child. They also do it by evoking a we-together feeling in the group as a whole, i.e. with the children among themselves and the teachers. In this connection, the New Zealand researcher Margaret Brennan (2005) speaks of a 'culture of tenderness': teachers who, with love, patience, homour and personal attention, help young children to feel at home and join into the rhythm and rules of the group. How do teachers do this?

Greeting: evoking the you-belong-feeling

Sharon (2;11) comes in holding her father's hand. She immediately goes up to Siglin, the teacher, who is sitting on a large chair at a table with other children. 'Hello, Sharon,' says Siglin, 'is your mummy better? Can you come to the crèche again today?' Siglin regards Sharon in a very friendly manner. She is sitting at Sharon's eye level and draws her loosely toward her in a greeting. The father stands by the door smiling and looks around him. Then he looks again at Siglin and his daughter. Siglin asks him: 'Is your wife better?' Sharon's father nods. Siglin sees him hesitate and asks if he'd like to come and sit with them; but he has no time and so says goodbye to his daughter. After the waving goodbye ritual Sharon goes and sits on Siglin's lap. Siglin goes on talking to the other children: 'Nat, are you going to Suriname this summer?' Nat nods. 'And you, Megan, where are you going?' Siglin asks the children what they are doing at home, constantly using

Vivianne throws sand at Quintly

Questioning look: is it allowed?

Sail away, sail away

their names when she speaks to them individually and in so doing involves all the children in the conversation.

Watching the children quietly

The children are playing outside with sand. They shovel their moulds full of sand, then empty them again, they grab each other's mould and take it back again. The teacher sits on the edge of the sandpit and watches the way the children play. She observes the way the children make clear to each other what they want and what they have discovered. In this way, she forms her plans for new activities to offer them, an extension of what they are already doing off their own bat.

Responding to the children's social referencing

Vivianne (2;7), Bojan (3;9) and Quintly (3;11) play with the sand table. Then, with a smile on her face, Vivianne throws a bit of sand in Bojan's direction and immediately looks in the direction of the teacher and the camerawoman. The camerawoman doesn't react and the teacher is occupied elsewhere. Vivianne now takes a large shovel-full and with a beaming smile throws it straight into Bojan's face. Quintly comes to his friend's defence: 'Don't do that, Vivianne!' But Vivianne now throws a shovel-full of sand at Quintly and ducks away in anticipation of the sand she expects back. Quintly pulls an unhappy face and glances quickly toward the camerawoman. Again, there is no reaction from the camerawoman. Quintly now throws a hefty charge of sand at Vivianne. Now the children scream in excitement. When children see that a teacher of an adult is looking at them and does not interfere, they assume that what they are doing is fine and become ever wilder. In this case of the sand-throwing incident, the teacher has to react: in a friendly way but making it very clear that this is not allowed.

Over the sandbanks

Sevgi explains

Everyone looks

Playing all together

Marysol, the teacher, sits on the ground with a baby and Seyen (2;8) both together on her lap. She is playing 'aeroplanes'. For a while, Rodney (2;6) looks on with interest. Then Marysol holds up her hand: 'Come on, Rodney, now you come in my aeroplane.' Shaya (2;3) then quickly comes over, having picked up the scent of fun and games. 'What is it Shaya-papaya?' asks Marysol. 'Do you want to come with us too? Come on then' and she lifts Shaya on to her lap. All four children are now sitting on Marysol's lap and then they all shout: 'Hold tight!'

The aeroplane then changes into a boat. 'Sailing, sailing, over the sandbanks,' the children sway with Marysol from left to right and love it. 'Oi!' Marysol sways too far to the right and the boat lists heavily. Laughing, the children tumble over one another. 'The boat is sinking!' they shout. 'Once more! Once more!' shout the children. And there they go again.

Levels of interaction between teacher and children

Within the group of children at a day-care centre one can distinguish different levels of interaction and social relations. At all these levels, the teacher has a direct or indirect influence on the quality of communal play and cooperation.

Teacher – child: with a young child this is the basic relationship. It is therefore very important that the teacher relates to each child individually and develops a personal relationship.

(Teacher) – child – child: at this level the teacher's role is to support the communal play of a small group of children.

Teacher – group of children: at this level it is more a matter of togetherness among the children as a group.

Pedagogical tips to remember

Teacher – child

- Each morning when she greets them (and also saying goodbye) the teacher gives all her attention to each child in turn. There are two things she lets them see:

  1. 'I'm glad you're here.' She can do this by smiling, touching, giving a cuddle, addressing the child by name or by engaging with the parent in an open, hearty fashion.

  2. 'We are all familiar with each other. I know who you are, I know your mummy and daddy and I know who you like to play with, what you like to do, what are the important events in your life and what your plans are for today.' The teacher does this by chatting with the par-

ents and talking with the child about yesterday or today, commenting on the new trousers or frock they're wearing etc. She can also help the child begin with the day's first activities, either alone or with other children.

- If the child has to do something during a group activity, but doesn't want to, the teacher makes a personal, friendly joke of the situation to show that she has the child's interest at heart.

(Teacher) – child – child

The teacher remains highly important during communal play with other children.

- The teacher is close at hand and watches the children attentively. She takes the time to observe without interfering.

- The questioning look. Toddlers regularly cast a glance toward the teacher when they are playing together. Eye contact reassures the children that they psychologically feel at home together. Children mainly look when they are uncertain or want help, but they also look to read the teacher's face, to see whether she is still attending to them, whether something is right or wrong and when something is exciting or dangerous. By means of eye contact the teacher can show that she is there for the child and can guide the child's behaviour. A disapproving look is sufficient for many children to stop, whereas most children will interpret a lack of any reaction as approval. It is therefore very important for a teacher to pay full attention to children while they are engaged in free play: both for their sense of security and of being accepted, and as a guardian of the boundaries between right and wrong and between safe and dangerous.

- Playing together with the children, either to enrich their play or to get them started.
  This latter is particularly important with young children and with children who are new to the group. The teacher can enrich children's play by telling stories that inspire them to let's-pretend-games, drawing or building constructions.

- Giving the children the chance to care for each other, letting them help comfort an unhappy child, or getting them to send a drawing to a child who is ill. Encourage older children to help little ones with games or putting coats on etc. Encourage children to help with the clearing up.

- When there are arguments or quarrels, intervene so that children can restore relations and learn the necessary skills to find solutions for themselves.

- Playing together is important because it gives the teacher the opportunity, always in a playful manner, to use and articulate in words the rules of reciprocity.

Teacher-children's group

In this context, the teacher can foster the feeling of togetherness between children in the group and ensure an environment that will elicit play.

- We-together-play, celebrations and enacting rituals. We-together-play is play in which all the children can participate and which evokes a strong feeling of belonging and togetherness through communal action and the pleasure it brings. Examples include music-making, singing, reciting rhymes, dancing, gym exercises, talking together in a circle, sitting with a group of children on a mattress and reading to them, birthday rituals, children from the after-school care centre giving a circus performance for the young ones, the teachers and parents, or celebrating the annual Christmas party together.
  To engender a positive we-feeling within the whole group it is important that the children participate of their own free will. It doesn't matter if they wander off or do something else as long as this does not disturb the other children. There has to be room for the part-together-part-alone behaviour that is so characteristic of children under the age of four.

- Thinking up pet-names can also enhance the feeling of togetherness. In the example above, the teacher Marysol calls Shaya Shaya-Papaya. We also heard Andy-Pandy or Dennis-the-Menace.

- Teachers indirectly exert an enormous influence through routines and the daily rhythm, and by structuring the space and the play materials. This will be the subject of the following chapter.

9   How teachers elicit and guide play

The teacher is also the group's stage manager. Staying with this theatrical metaphor for a moment, we can say: she knows that the actors (the children) will create the play themselves, and that for this they need to be given free rein. But she also gives new impulses by participating in the play and by giving the actors stage directives. She makes sure the decor and the necessary props are all there to elicit specific play; in both direct and indirect ways she structures the being-together of the children (Jones & Reynolds, 1992).

Everyone cooperates

After the morning snack the children are invited to help clear and tidy up the dining area. There are little brooms and dustpans with long handles to sweep up crumbs and any rubbish. Marysol shows several children how they have to hold a broom. Lots of children want to help but there is one broom too few. Marysol offers to go and find another, but this takes too long for Bert (2;11). He tries to grab one of the other children's brooms and bursts into angry tears. Bill's mother sees this happening. This morning, Bill (2;1) is with the group for only the second time to get used to it. 'Look, Bill,' says his mother, 'your friend's crying! You should help him. Go and help your friend. Give him the broom.' Bill looks around hesitantly, but then gives the broom to Bert. He quickly runs back to his mother who gives him a cuddle. 'I'm proud of you. You helped your friend!' Bill then goes off in search of something else, finds a dustpan and joins in again with the group of 'working' children.

Everyone cooperates

Marysol shows them how you hold the broom

Playing shops

Ritva, a teacher in a Finnish day-care centre, goes to play with Iida (3;3), Anni (2;6), Mari (2;4) and Katju (1;11) in the sleeping space. Apart from beds and some chairs there is a single large clothes cupboard with doors. Ritva has previously constructed a shop with shopping bags, a weighing scale, empty milk cartons, Brinta, sugar, coffee, tea, biscuits and suchlike. She goes to sit on a large chair by her 'shop'. 'Look at all the things you can buy in the shop. Are you going to do your shopping?' The children immediately pick up on this, they put their shopping in a bag and bring it to the clothes cupboard and creep inside. Only Katju, the youngest, appears hesitant. 'What are you going to buy?' asks the teacher, at which Katju takes something and creeps into the clothes cupboard with the others. A simple game is repeated several times: the children fetch their shopping from the shop and take it 'home', then bring it back to the shop in order to 'buy' it once again. The teacher then suggests to Iida, the eldest child, that she buys something special to surprise the other children at home. By means of such a directive the teacher is able to inject a new impulse into their play. There is a balance between the teacher's direction and that of the children (Hännikäinen, 1997).

Pedagogical tips to remember

The teacher has at her disposal various means of directing the activities and play of the children in her care. If the aim of her direction is to facilitate togetherness among the children, the following points are worth considering:

- *Routines*. Fixed activities performed together at particular times of the day, such as the circle, clearing up, eating, sleeping or singing. It is important in these routines to appeal to young children's natural inclination to seek proximity and to imitate. There should also be room for personal contributions by the children and the possibility for them to influence the routine. If there is one thing that is unsuitable for young children it is group discipline!

All building together

Hurrah! the tower is finished

Please sir, who is going to do the shopping now?

- *Working together*. Young children like doing things together with adults. They love to help at home when mother changes the bed or washes up. When the teacher sets down the plates or cutlery there's good chance that children will ask 'Can I do it too?' Two- and three-year-olds love to make plans together: for example, how they can surprise someone or what they are going to make or do together.

- *Playing together*. One and two-year-olds often still need a teacher to give them directions, explain things and indicate what is allowed and what not. This is best done by playing with them, letting them go their own way and giving guidance and input as necessary, having already a good grasp of the logic of the children's play/game.

  When children understand what building a tower is, or playing make-believe, they are perfectly capable of playing without a teacher and are able to stimulate each other with fresh input. The teacher can enrich the play of older children too, by telling stories, acting out stories together or involving the children in games with glove-puppets or puppet-shows. She can also give the children information on stereotypical roles in a game of make-believe. There are undoubtedly also other teachers who, like Ritva – the Finnish teacher in our example, can elicit make-believe games but we hardly ever saw it in our research in Dutch day-care centres.

- *Arranging the space and the play materials*. To invite playing-together, the teacher can create an environment in which:

  - both outside and inside there is room to romp and run around without disturbing others;

  - there is room to play quietly alone or with a few other children;

  - there are corners where materials elicit a particular game;

  - there are thematic props available to suggest make-believe games;

  - there is not an overload of materials, so that they can be regularly changed to surprise the children with something new;

  - one can take account of what children need at any particular moment: a corner with water and sand, small and larger building materials – which all lead to other forms of playing-together.

Part 2

NEWCOMERS

10 From outsider to member of the club

When teachers and children give concrete form to their 'being-together', they do this by observing each other well, by doing things together, by playing and talking together – in short, by being with each other in *particular* ways. They construct a way of being together that one could call the group's *culture*. Each child, and also the teacher, makes his or her own contribution. Everyone gives form to certain patterns of mixing with each other. Many of these things are so self-evident that they are never given a moment's thought.

For a newcomer, however, it's a quite a job to discover the ways of a group. They are mainly tacit, unspoken – and fortunately so, since it would all be too much to actually remember! In fact it's hard work learning the rules of a group. By far the majority of children very much want to belong and they work hard at it; they keep their eyes and ears open and gradually assimilate the rules and perhaps later even add rules themselves. The teachers too have to work hard at it. In all childcare centres there are routines for letting the children find their feet. It is also important to let the parents familiarise themselves and to gain their confidence. To some extent they will always remain outsiders, but in as far as they are inside they belong there with their experience and their desires. It's good for them to get to learn the culture of the group and, vice versa, it's good for the teacher to know something of the parents' culture.

The following chapters are an invitation to look with new children at all the rules and procedures in the group, to see how new children join in and to look with parents at how they and their children can form part of the 'club'.

The researcher who wants to belong

In 1983 William Corsaro, the American known for his research on the lives of American children, was commissioned to carry out a research project in the Italian city of Bologna. He began his research at a child day-care centre while at the same time trying to learn Italian. He describes how after a month he understood far more of what the children did and did not do, but also how he always felt that he was an outsider (Corsaro, 1988; 1997). One day he had a breakthrough. He was sitting with two small boys, Felice and Roberto, who were playing with their toy racing cars and heard one of them say: 'Lui e` morto.' Understanding that this meant 'He is dead', he remembered a phrase from his Italian lessons and said: 'Che peccato!' (What a pity!). Felice and Robert looked at him in amazement. 'Bill! Bill! Ha ragione!' (He's right!) shouted Felice excitedly: 'Bravo, Bill!' applauded Roberto: 'Bravo, Bill!' Felice then called the other children over and recounted to them the story of Bill, who could now say 'Che peccato'. The children were extremely pleased at this and some went so far as to clap him. 'I felt good', writes Corsaro, 'like one of the group.' But although he was no longer the outsider, he remained a rather singular member of the club. Because of his inadequate Italian it seemed that children sometimes doubted his abilities and sometimes mocked him: 'Bill, lui capice niente!' (Bill, he doesn't understand anything!). It was for him a new experience and he realized that what had happened to him was happening all the time the other way round: that adults simply don't see that children have their own forms of doing things and being together; and so they often assume that children can't do things. His work is especially aimed at showing how children have their own ways of dealing with each other and how they develop their own culture. The experience of being a newcomer and having to find his own way in an unfamiliar environment certainly stood him in good stead.

11 New to the group

When children are new the parents come with them to help them get accustomed and to help the teachers make the children feel safe and at home. If necessary they explain, they give them extra cuddles and they pay close attention to how things go. But the new child him- or herself is actively trying to understand everything and how to relate to these other children. Carmen Dalli, a New Zealand academic, has investigated the way children accustom themselves to such new situations. The following story of Robert is taken from her work. Robert was 26 months old when he was placed in a day-care centre. According to Laurien, his teacher, Robert was a dominant boy who quickly found his feet among the other children. 'He paid attention to the other children, even in tiny things. He never ran into other children, or took things from them. He seemed to know what he could and couldn't do in order to avoid other children getting angry with him.' According to the teacher, Robert seemed almost automatically to accustom himself to the other children. But the video-recordings enabled Dalli to see how Robert so rapidly learned what you should do and not do in order to remain good friends.

Rules on ownership and sharing the toys of the day-care centre

From the first moment that Robert appeared with his mother in the group, he sought contact with the other children. He learned the group rules for relating to other children through minor conflicts; for example, the rules for who could play with which toys or objects. The first rules over ownership that he learned were probably the following:
Rule: If I take an object from someone, he will take it back.
Rule: If someone claims an object back, I can do this too.

Wim seeks

and finds Suzanne

Rule: Whoever has the object first may continue playing with it, and will be upheld by the teacher.

8:32	Robert sits at the table playing with animal figures. Nancy, on Robert's left, stands up from her chair and Robert immediately pulls her chair toward him. Nancy claims her chair back. The teacher says nothing.
10:38	Robert and the teacher stand in the dressing-up corner. Nancy arrives with the helicopter that Robert had been playing with earlier. Robert reaches toward the helicopter and takes it from Nancy. Nancy tries to grab it back again, but she is then led off. Robert goes with the helicopter to his mother. Neither mother nor teacher say anything about the incident.

The second time that he comes to the day-care centre he learns a rule about ownership:

Rule: When there are several examples of one and the same kind of toy, it is best to take one that nobody is playing with.

12:10	Robert is playing with a toy truck in the vicinity of three other children. He looks at the much larger truck that Hugo is playing with. Robert now pushes a cart and with it approaches the large truck that Hugo has just got off. Hugo screams "My truck" and demands it back. Pam, the teacher, says, "Robert, do you want a truck too? Which do you want?" Robert chooses another large truck and takes this to where his mother is sitting.
12:31	Robert walks over to a group of children around Pam, who is reading to them. He sees the truck that Hugo had earlier been playing with and goes and sits on it to listen to the story.
12:33	Hugo walks up to the group of children, then goes toward Robert. Robert gets of the truck. Hilary, another teacher, gives Robert another large truck to sit on.

Rolling together

Sliding off the bench

In the last example, Robert immediately and of his own accord gave the truck back to Hugo. He seems to understand the rule of 'whoever was playing with an object earlier may keep it in his possession', but he does not always stick to this rule. During his third and fourth visits he appears to learn a new rule:

Rule: The law of the strongest.

10:15	Robert is sitting at the puzzle table. He looks up in the direction of the noise of the rocking horse that Bill is riding. Robert walks in Bill's direction and goes to sit on a beanbag near Bill's rocking horse. He reaches for another rocking horse which he pushes up and down from behind. Bill gets off his rocking horse, whereupon Robert immediately mounts it. Bill does not like this, protests and pulls the horse's ears. Robert says 'No, no' and sits firmly on the horse. Bill walks away.
8:03	Robert goes to the lego table, commandeers the chair of a younger child and proceeds to sit on it. The younger child accepts this under protest.

Robert has probably perceived that if you are stronger, and if the teacher is not around, you can do as you wish. During his fourth visit, however, he also learns the more civilised way of sharing scarce toys in the group:

Rule: If there is only one of a certain kind of toy this can be shared by taking turns to play with it. During his fourth visit he learns the taking-turns-rule from the teacher:

10:30	Robert looks at two children, Danny and Toby, who are playing together on the seesaw. When Toby gets off one end, Robert races up to the seesaw and sits on it. Toby cries as Robert t has his turn. 'It's Robert's turn now' says the teacher to Toby, 'You can have another go after Robert.' Toby is till crying in protest. Robert sees this. The teacher lifts Toby up and soothes him. Robert really enjoys the seesaw. A little later Danny gets off the seesaw and Robert stops too.

Co-construction: making rules together

In every group, rules are made about what is permitted, what is good and what is bad. Psychologists who follow in the footsteps of the pioneering Vygotsky, call this 'co-construction', where 'construction' refers to the fact that the rules are not naturally given but are made by people, and 'co-' refers to the fact that rules are always made together with other people. How one deals with the question of ownership and the sharing of valuable goods differs from one culture to another.

Children appropriate the culture in which they grow up; the rules that children make are for a large part determined by the values and norms of their parents and teachers. In the process, they are confronted with cultural differences. Moreover, teachers within Dutch culture can have different views over sharing together and what a child may keep. In a group, children put into practice what they have learned from their teachers and parents; but they do it in their own way and also make rules that their educators do not approve of, such as the law of the strongest.

Conflicts are occasions for learning

Robert learned very quickly in conflicts with other children what worked and what did not – through other children protesting, being stronger or appealing to the teacher. Robert showed himself to be most efficient in the learning process. In this way he learned social skills and the social rules of reciprocity of his group. He also learned the validity of the rule of the strongest if the teacher was not paying attention.

Pedagogical tips to remember

When there is a new child in the group you should keep a close watch on how communal play proceeds. If you see that the child wants to join in, go and sit with him or her and explain what the other children are doing and what their names are. Observe the way the child tries to make contact and what leads to clashes. You can then explain to the children what is going on, mediate and help the new child a little where necessary.

12 Making friends when you are not a native speaker

Finding your way in a new group is hard enough, but for a child who is not a native speaker it would seem to be a very difficult task. How do you make contact? How can you ensure that the others like playing with you? In her investigation of the way children who are learning a new language get to grips with this problem, Lilian Wong-Fillmore (1979) observed five children. She found that children employ a number of social strategies:
- You attach yourself to a group and behave as though you understand what's going on, even if you don't.
- Act as though you speak the language, by picking up and using a few words.
- Rely on your friends for help.

Making contact

Dounja (2;5), a little Moroccan girl, has recently joined a toddlers' group consisting of children from various cultural backgrounds. During free play she opts for the house corner. She stands next to the cooker. It's very busy there and other children want to play with things lying in Dounja's territory. Dounja's behaviour is entirely devoted to defending her 'domain'. She looks angry each time and shouts 'no' and 'aaah'. She manages to keep her things safe but certainly never gets as far as playing together with others. A week later we see that she has begun to understand that she must try another tack: during free play she has chosen to play with scissors and paste. She sits next to Hind, another Moroccan girl, who is tapping with a small hammer. Dounja wipes the glue to and fro over her paper, but is mainly busy looking

Hind laughs at Dounja in a comic fashion

Dounja laughs back in the same way

around her, especially at her neighbour. Then Hind grabs something from the bowl with stickers that stands next to Dounja and laughs at her, sticking her nose up in a comic fashion. This is the signal for Dounja to make contact. She laughs back at Hind in the same way and Hind in her turn makes the face again in a more exaggerated way. Hind is evidently much more interesting than cutting and pasting! The contact is made: Hind snorts at Dounja with her lips and Dounja promptly does the same back. After snorting at each other a few more times and having returned to their work again, Hind sings 'To?', upon which Dounja joins in until somewhat later they have jointly composed a 'To-song' that ends with couplets exchanged by Dounja and Hind. They have evidently found each other. They then discover that they have something else in common: Moroccan!

What follows is a game in which they repeat each other and then with variations. It is a potpourri of Moroccan words and sentences – *tila tila* (you, you), *tlaqqlie* (let me go), *waga habiba djeli* (yes, my dear) – nonsense-words (*pattòja pattòja*) that they construct out of Dutch and Morocccan sounds and Moroccan endings that they can extend to great length *(pattòjaaaaa, pattòjpattòjpattòja)*, and Dutch words that Dounja has taken over from Hind (*stout, stout-e-stout*). They are budding songwriters!

After a while a conflict arises when Dounja starts to bang on Hind's toy. The teacher then intervenes by directing Dounja back to her own work: 'Dounja, you can't bang on Hind's hammer, because you were pasting.'

Of course, it is important that the children themselves stay with their chosen occupation, but for children who are new to the group it can sometimes be more important that the teacher supports them in their quest for contact. In this case, for example, the teacher could have helped more by showing how they both could make the same patterns in their work. In that way a new sort of co-operation could develop while at the same time they would both finish their own task.

Hind snorts at Dounja

Dounja does the same back

Playing together is often playing with language

Playing together is also important for learning the language. In the language play of Dounja and Hind one can see that there is a lot of playing with sounds, with Dounja sometimes taking over words from Hind. In fact, playing together is often language play! Precisely because young children like to imitate each other it is a very good idea that a new child who speaks no English should play with another who can.* The desire to play together is a powerful motivating force to start the acquisition of English!

With children who are learning the language, teachers often pay more attention to content in what they say: they put questions, create space for the children themselves to talk and discuss the content of what the child says. They will often deliberately introduce new words and repeat them. Both are important when learning a new language (Peck, 1978).

Pedagogical tips to remember

Keep a close eye on how a child who doesn't speak English – or whatever the language of the daycare centre – tries to find her way amongst other children and make sure there is a warm 'language bath'.

- Make sure you have much personal contact where you talk about what you are doing together at the time and about the things you are using. When you are specially attending to the child you will note that your own language use is simpler than normal. Joining the child in his or her play activities will give numerous opportunities to use words for what you are doing together. This attention to and naming of the things the child is absorbed with is very important.

- Make sure that you allow the child enough room to talk, but at the same time be aware that (s)he needs time to understand the language.

- Group talks in the wider circle are a waste of time for new children who do not speak English language; they feel totally isolated. Much better is to have small circles if there are more teachers in the group: it's much more intimate. Within such a group too, address the child personally. A small group and individual contact also make it easier for the children themselves to speak.

- Repetition is of course very important. Use the daily routines every time as an opportunity to emphasise the words that are important in each situation. Exaggerate in the repetition!

---

* In the text it will be assumed that English is the native language spoken at the daycare centre.

- In all activities, think what are the relevant words that a child needs: constantly name things and in doing so give special attention to a number of words that you want the child to learn.

And to continue from the strategies of Wong-Fillmore:

- As soon as children have the correct words, they can begin to make friends with them.

- Try to find for the child a language-mate with the same mother language and who is further ahead with learning English. Give the language-mate special language tasks that will draw in the child whose English is less developed: 'Dounja, will you explain what you have to do?'

13 Making parents and children welcome

Good contact between parents and teachers has a positive effect on all concerned. The child feels secure, the parent can leave the child behind with an easy mind and the teacher can do her best work.

A partnership between parents and teachers is the basis for children's proper development; it also underpins the development of their identity. Who am I? I belong in a family and I have a place in this group at the day-care centre. Good contact between teachers and parents gives children a feeling of safety. If you take something from home to the centre and if something from the centre is brought home, this creates the connection for the child, there is continuity. The partnership between parents and teachers begins when the parents are made welcome, when they are made to feel that they belong there. Making someone welcome is an active process initiated by the teacher and the day-care centre. For instance, they can ask themselves: When do parents feel welcome? How can teachers facilitate this? In De Graaff's study of parental involvement and diversity, parents and teachers give their own accounts of their experience (Graaff & Keulen, 2007).

A mother:

> 'It's nice if the teachers make contact when I go in, if they address you by name, it makes it personal. I don't really have to talk about what I myself have been doing today, but I do like to hear if my children have done something special. Making you welcome doesn't necessarily need words. You know that they've seen you.'

A father relates his experience of bringing and fetching his child:

> 'Because I don't know the parents' and children's names I often act the jolly fellow, even when I'm not. I'm insecure. Because I don't know most people there and I forget names. Sometimes also because the teachers stand there waiting, like posts in a corner, and also because the children are coming in. The teachers could make me feel more welcome, you know. And sometimes it happens. sometimes there's a teacher who strikes a warmer note. She says 'Good morning' in a really friendly way, especially to the children; then you can be a normal father. She doesn't need to talk to me, as long as there's a welcoming atmosphere. That's nice. Then it's as if the ice is broken and you can enjoy it all normally. Then it's fine to leave your child behind.'

Mother:

'I feel happy if I know that my son is having a good time. When he sees the teacher it's always, ha! Then I think, like: I can leave him with an easy mind. I'm more or less happy with all the teachers. The most important thing is that I leave him behind feeling confident. It comes from giving children real attention, calling them by name, asking them how they are. They know it's always a bit difficult for me saying goodbye; when I leave they always take him on their lap and give him the necessary attention.'

Mother:

'It has to be spontaneous, I think that's also important. That's what I like with these teachers. Then I'm happy and I express that, because I know they look after my child very well. Yes, really well. That gives me a feeling of calm. When I go away I feel guilty and sad but my mind is at ease. My child was unwell today and then I know they'll look after him properly. Honest, no question.'

These parents indicate that feeling welcome, or finding it easy to leave their child behind at a day-care centre, is a matter of small things. Parents sometimes feel uncertain or guilty even, but they don't always show it!

Making parents welcome with a
family wall

A teacher makes father feel welcome
at an admissions talk

A teacher tells how she makes parents feel welcome:

'When parents come with their children, I make them really welcome. The children all first do a puzzle with their parents or do something on the table. Meanwhile you chat with the parents, with one or the other just to give them the feeling that they're welcome. It's the same when you say goodbye: you wish them a good weekend, you know, little things, that's what counts.'

Another teacher who has just been giving an admission talk:

'In an admission talk you try to tell them everything that's important. I like to do it well and not leave anything out. I was a bit worried for her so I just took the mother round the group: we're doing this here, that there. You could see the mother being satisfied. For example, she asked questions. She was from Ghana, I spoke English with her.'

There are many ways of extending a welcome; with a wink or a smile, with questions that show interest or with a story about an experience the child has had. There are some methods to help you put questions or start a conversation, like the 'welcome sun' or the 'family wall'.

The partnership between parents and teachers begins with extending a welcome to the parents, giving them the feeling that they belong there. Conversations can then naturally develop over experiences at home or in the childcare centre. This kind of conversation needs an atmosphere of trust and respect for everyone's expertise and responsibilities, the parents for the teacher's and the teacher for the parents'.

- Make active contact with the parents when they bring and fetch their child. It doesn't have to be done with words, it can be as little as a wink, a smile or a wave of the hand.

- Always assume that the parents know their child best. They deal with the child every day. Ask parents how things go at home with the child: how do they get him or her to sleep, how they comfort the child, how do they eat together. Ask them too what they find important in the day-care centre. What would they themselves like to see teachers doing?

- If there are mothers with different mother languages, a good way of welcoming them in is to hang a welcome sun at entrance: a large sun with the word 'welcome' in different languages across the sun's rays. You can ask the parents to add a 'welcome' in their own language.

- The family wall is a method of making both parents and children welcome.
  Photographs of each child in its family situation are hung on the wall: photos of the parents, of a granny who looks after the child or an aunt, but pets too – the dog or a guinea-pig. The family wall gives children and parents the feeling: 'I belong here and I can be myself, just as I am.' Differences in life-style or family structure are both visible and accepted.

Part 3

CLASHES AND SQUABBLES

14 Clashes are relational work

When children play together there are of course quarrels. They irritate each other, they both want or find something different, or they get really angry. Teachers and parents often find this tiresome. Crying, angry or whining children – we'd all much rather see them playing happily together without conflict. Developmental psychologists, however, think very differently about conflicts between children (Piaget, 1967; Vygotsky, 1978). They find them highly important for a child's development.

In groups, quarrels have the function of clarifying relationships between members of the group: what is allowed, what is not, who is the boss and who must obey, what are the rules for sharing together and what you are allowed to keep for yourself (De Waal, 2000). Research has shown that young children, just as adults, are concerned not only with what they want (the content) but also with how they can influence the other (the relationship) or how to restore the relationship after a conflict (Verbeek, Hartup & Collins, 2000; Singer, 2002). This is why conflicts are relational work. When young children do something that they probably shouldn't do, they often look round with a vague, anticipatory naughty–child little smile, as though to mollify their parents or teacher. And if the parent or teacher is angry nonetheless, they often start crying, wanting to be comforted and reconciled.

Children of a very young age are already capable of finding solutions when they get into quarrels with each other: the stronger the desire to play together, the greater the chance of finding a solution acceptable to both sides. They also make it very plain if they don't like another child. Research among young children shows that, during a conflict, they employ various strategies to restore, to clarify or to break off relations. Sometimes they get involved in quarrels between two other children. Even with toddlers, conflicts constitute work on relationships. This is what we too found in our own research, and this is the subject of the following chapter.

15 Clashes between young children

By a 'clash' we mean a situation in which a child does something at which another child protests. This definition already implies that these clashes can be of very brief duration if the first child immediately ceases his attempt to get something done. But clashes can also last much longer. So we decided in our research to make a distinction between three kinds of clash of different levels of seriousness:

1. Mishaps, minor incidents in which the 'victim' reacts instantaneously to a push or a punch, or when another child takes his toy, and where the clash ends with that reaction. We call these incidents 'mishaps' because we assume that the children think that they just happened to have had bad luck. Although in many cases the teacher won't even notice such minor incidents, close observation of video-recordings allows one to see that a series of mishaps can lead to mounting irritation and even to a full-blown row.

   Keenan (2;1) is playing at the table with farm animals. Bart (3;5) wanders around and comes to stand next to Keenan. He looks at the animals that Keenan is playing with. Bart reaches out a hand toward one of the animals on the table. Keenan looks at Bart, shouts 'No' and pushes his arm away. Bart walks away from the table and goes to play somewhere else.

2. Disagreements, or conflicts of will, when children persevere for some time with their own idea, resisting the other's proposal until one of the two gives in, gives up or a compromise is found.

Rinesh wants something from Lilly's doctor's bag

No, bad luck

Why not?

Kristel (2;10) and Melissa (3;5) are playing with toy cutlery and fruit. Kristel divides up the fruit. Melissa points to a pear lying on a little pan and says 'Pear'. Kristel then holds up another pear, looks at Melissa and asks: 'Pear?' Melissa shakes her head and says: 'No, no, that one, that one' and taps the pear against the one lying in the pan. Kristel lays her pear in the pan with the other pear. Melissa again points to the pan and says: 'Put it here apple too.' To which Kristel replies: 'You mustn't eat that.' Melissa asks: 'Why not?' and at the same time pokes an orange. 'Because we're going to sing first!' calls Kristel. Melissa catches on and calls in a singing tone: 'We're going to sing!' Kristel and Melissa continue playing together with the fruit.

3. Full-blown row, where children show strong emotional reactions, with angry words or crying - reactions which indicate that, for at least one of the children, the limit of toleration has been breached.

Miriam (3;4) is playing with large wooden blocks on the ground beside the sofa. First she puts several blocks on the sofa and then she uses them to build a tower. When she turns round she observes that a few of the blocks that were previously on the sofa are now lying on the ground. She puts them back on the sofa and continues building. Very soon there are more blocks lying beside the sofa! By chance, Tijmen (2;4) comes up at this moment. Miriam assumes that it was Tijmen who must have thrown the blocks from the sofa. She steps up to him and gives him a hard clout on the back of the head with one of the large wooden blocks, at which Tijmen cries out in pain. Joke (3;9) who is sitting on the bank and has been all the time throwing the blocks off, looks on aghast.

How often do clashes occur?

Research carried out in the United States, in various European countries and in Japan, has shown that, during free play, two- and three-year-old children have on average 5 to 8 clashes per hour (Shantz,1987; Singer & Hännikäinen, 2002). In our own research we found 12 clashes per hour. This higher frequency of clashes in Dutch childcare centres is partly a problem of definition

That's how it should be!   Urjandric wants the doll   No, you can't do that!

– what we understand in our research as a 'clash'. We include minor irritations or 'mishaps' which may not always have been included in other investigations. If we exclude the very minor clashes, we come out with 7 clashes per hour which, compared with other countries, appears to be still rather on the high side. The number of rows is also relatively high at one per hour. Clashes between young children are brief, on average not longer than 18 seconds.

Table 1: Number of clashes per hour at child day-care centres or toddlers' playrooms and their duration					
	Mishaps	Disagreements	Rows	Total number of clashes	Average duration
Number per hour	5	6	1	12	
Duration in seconds	7	23	54		18

The question of whether children in our childcare centres clash too much is not easily susceptible to a simple answer. Mishaps are not serious, but when such minor incidents recur frequently this does suggest that children are getting in each other's way and irritating each other. Rows can be major moments of learning for children, but hitting and kicking make children feel insecure with each other. We shall return to this question in Part 5, on the role of teachers.

16 Relational work

Both from our own work and research in other countries it is clear that young children resolve most of their clashes without a teacher. In 79 percent of the clashes recorded in our research, no teacher was involved. In fact, children often continue playing as though nothing has happened. Perhaps the continuation of the play is more important to them than getting their own way; or perhaps young children forget what is going on as soon as their attention is seized by something else. They can also achieve resolution by softening their behaviour and becoming reconciled. They can offer a toy, laugh, pull silly faces, concede or propose that they go on playing.

Laughing

Leo (2;2) grasps for the building work of Farchat (3;8). Farchat shouts: 'Hey, hey, leave it alone.' He tries to save his building by grabbing Leo's arm and then his building work. He shouts 'Aaah!' and tries to go on with his building work. Then he says 'hmmm,' after which he looks at Leo, laughing. Leo laughs back at Farchat and the two boys then continue playing together.

Practising magic together

Khalid (3;7) says: 'I put a magic spell on Sanne so she disappears,' while at the same time waving his hat like a magic wand. Sanne (3;11) says: 'No, you can't do that.' Khalid persists: 'Yes, I can, you go that side,'and grabs Sanne's hand. Sanne then makes a proposition: 'No, no, let's do magic together.' And on this suggestion Khalid and Sanne cast their magic spells together.

Who is the strongest?

Maybe the camerawoman will help

Then I'll get it back

Just concede and then try again?

Jan (3;1) is highly interested in the xylophone that Bert (3;11) is playing with. Bert wanders through the playroom, occasionally sitting down, and beating the xylophone with a stick, while Jan follows him, watching. Jan also has a stick and when Bert isn't watching, Jan quickly strikes the xylophone. But the sound betrays him. Bert quickly snatches the xylophone away from Jan. Jan stops at once and withdraws a little until he sees a new chance. Bert sometimes reacts by pulling an angry face, saying 'No, no' and pushing Jan away. Then he seems just to ignore Jan and to accept the fact that Jan touches the xylophone.

This game of having a try (Jan), resisting or reacting crossly (Bert), withdrawing (Jan), taking every subsequent chance to strike the xylophone once again (Jan) and conceding (Bert) is repeated many times over a period of some twenty minutes.

Conceding

Sylvano (3;4) stands in a play-house, jumping up and down and singing a song. Rafik (3;4) begins to scream that Sylvano must stop. He tries to get Sylvano to be quiet but at the same time he wants to be his friend: 'I am your friend, aren't I?' he says. 'Yes, but then you have to sing a song too' replies Sylvano and starts singing the song again and jumping up and down. Rafik looks thoughtfully at Sylvano but eventually joins in the singing and jumping in the playhouse.

Communication: the message and the relationship

What do you want and what do I want? Who is the boss? Do we like each other? In their clashes, children – like everybody else – communicate on two levels.
1. At the level of the verbal message, there is the content (what you want the other to do or not do). In our examples: stay away from my building project (Farchat); I don't want you to put a disappearing-spell on me (Sanne); I want to play on the xylophone too (Jan); keep off (Bert). We shall look further at this level of the verbal content in Part 4.

This is Britt and Joris. They are friends   Sometimes they get angry for instance when Joris wants to grab Britt's ball   They are soon friends again; Britt holds the ball behind her back – a joke!

2. At the relational level (how the child appraises the other), there are two aspects to the appraisal of a relationship:
   – Dominance and submission (whether the child thinks he can boss the other around and the other should obey - and vice versa, the submissive role). When both children behave equally dominantly, or when each takes the other's wishes into consideration, we presume that there is a power-relationship between the children which they both accept. An example of the latter is the clash between Khalid and Sanne over the disappearing-spell. Khalid takes Sanne into account and she gives reasons why she does or doesn't want something. In the example of Bert and Jan with the xylophone, Bert is the dominant one: he has the xylophone and makes no attempt to persuade Jan with explanations or to mitigate Jan's frustrations by laughing or joking. Out of irritation, Bert simply ignores Jan, while Jan appears to accept Bert's dominance in this confrontation: he does not try to seize the xylophone, but he does try to take his chances within the limits set by Bert.
   – Friendly or hostile (whether the child has positive or negative feelings toward the other). In the first example, Farchat makes it very clear that he does not want his building work destroyed (the verbal content), but almost immediately, by laughing at him he lets it be known that he accepts Leo as a person and values him positively. Farchat eases the conflict by communicating positively over their relationship. With Leo's returned laugh, Farchat and Leo are reconciled with each other. Young children have difficulty in combining a verbal message of negative content (keep off my blocks) with a positive communication over the relationship (through a friendly tone, smiles). Adults are much better at this. A teacher, for example, can make it clear in a single sentence that she is the authority figure (dominant) and that hitting and kicking are not allowed (the negative verbal message) while at the same time through her positive tone and serious facial expression she shows that she has confidence in the child and that the relationship is not damaged (friendliness). Where adults can thus communicate both positive and negative messages in a single integrated form, children often give consecutive, opposite messages: first angrily making it clear that they don't want something and a little later propitiating the other with a laugh and offering something.

The relationship determines the issue: winning, giving up or reconciliation

'The closer and more positive the relationship, the greater the tendency to restore the relationship after a conflict' (Singer, 2002). This 'law of reconciliation' also applies to the case of clashes between young children. In our research we were not in a position to distinguish reliably between children who were good friends and children who were not really friends. We could, however, draw a clear distinction between clashes of children either playing together or in parallel and clashes of children who had been playing separately. (see table 2):

- When children were previously playing together, they often play together after the clash.
- When children were playing apart before their clash, they often also play apart afterwards.

As far as this is concerned, it makes no difference whether the teacher intervenes in the clash or not. When children have been playing together, it seems that they are so strongly motivated to go on playing together that even a row need not necessarily cause them to break off their play.

Table 2: Relation between initial situation and outcome of a clash.		
	Outcome	
Initial situation	*Playing alone*	*Playing together and parallel play*
Playing alone	79 %	21 %
Playing alone (with intervention by teacher)	81 %	19 %
Playing together and parallel play (with intervention by teacher)	20 %	80 %
Samenspel en parallelspel (met interventie leidster)	22 %	78 %

Pedagogical tips to remember

If you see a clash between two children and there is no immediate danger, do nothing:

- See how the children themselves tackle it. Is there a dominant child or are they equally matched? Is their attitude toward each other positive or negative?

- How is the clash eventually resolved? Children learn through practical experience with each other.

- Consider what you can do – if the situation arises again – in the way of explaining or offering to help the children take a step forward.

17 Champion of 'coercive seduction'

Many children in the toddlers' group have already acquired the communicative capacity to make clear what they want (verbal content). In direct contact with other children, they also understand the latter's feelings and wishes and know how to persuade, manipulate or propitiate them (the relationship). When they want something that they know the other does not want, they are capable of behaving according to the rule: 'Make sure you are nice if you want something.' Some of them have a whole repertoire of verbal and nonverbal resources available for their work on relations.

Jim (2;0) has brought his fire-engine into the group and Otto (3;10) finds it simply splendid. As soon as Jim puts in on the ground to play with it, Otto crawls up to him and says: 'I'm a fireman too' 'No,' replies Jim and clasps the fire-engine to his back. Otto tries again in a sweet voice: 'Can't we both be firemen?' He bends further forward and looks at Jim questioningly. But Jim is adamant: 'No, I want it myself,' and crawls away. Otto's opening gambit has been unsuccessful, even though it was such a smart move. He is aware that in order to get something from the other, you have to emphasise that you have something in common that makes it attractive for the other to share the desired object with you. Strengthen the relationship by letting it be known that you too belong to the firemen's club and you may get your wish, Otto knows this. But Jim, alas, wants first to be the sole fireman. Otto's timing has not been so good. Otto crawls after Jim and after a short pursuit tries to snatch the fire-engine out of Jim's hands. After a few attempts he looks inquiringly toward the teacher, but she is busy elsewhere. He then continues with his furious attempts to get hold of

Can't we both be firemen?

No, I want it myself and Jim crawls away

Otto tries to grab the fire-engine

the fire-engine by force. There is a back and forth tug-o-war, but Jim is the stronger.

After the failure of his first strategy, Otto is apparently so overwhelmed by his lust for the fire-engine that he loses sight of the good relationship with Jim. But his attack does not have the desired effect, and as soon as Otto realises this he switches to a third approach:

'I can, I can, can I have a go? I can have a go. Can one go. One go. One go. One go. One go.' Meanwhile he throws an arm round Jim's neck and half hangs on to him. When Jim tries to crawl away, Otto tries to stay in his field of vision and gives him an imploring look. Jim does not relent. As soon as Otto realises that imploring won't help either he tries once again to seize the fire-engine 'Don't do that Otto,' says another child playing nearby, and then another child also says: 'Don't do that Otto.' Evidently Otto has no support. By two years of age, children already have insight into the failure of their strategy and can review their behaviour.

Otto's repertoire is still not exhausted. Once more he ostensibly plays the card of togetherness: 'Together, together, together. We can play together, we can ...' Jim again moves away. Otto pursues him and when Jim sets the siren going, all Otto can do is to look. There then follows another sequence of attempts by Otto to seize the fire-engine, but Jim does not give in. Otto lets go, sulks and then begins once more with his: 'Together, can play together, can play together, can play together, we can play together, can't we? (now with emphasis), play together can't we, CAN'T WE!? In the meantime he has now managed to embrace the crawling Jim in such a way that he is now lying underneath him and has his face almost pressed against that of Jim, so that his coercive requests can no longer be avoided. But even now Jim goes on playing unperturbed with his fire-engine. One last echo: 'Can play together. Together ...'

Finally Otto realises that 'together' doesn't work. It is clear that for Otto, in this context, 'together' means above all 'now me'. Perhaps the teacher has used this rule in an earlier conflict over toys and Otto has understood that 'together' means 'taking your turn' or 'everyone can have a go'.

Can play together, can't we?   Under the teacher's watchful gaze....   Otto can play with the fire-engine too

When Jim again crawls away Otto tries: 'Me now, my turn? Me now? It's my turn, I can have a go now, I had my turn too? I can have a go, me too a go? Just one? One go? One, one go? Gi'me one go. Just one go.' Otto's sentences vary from questions to assertions to demands and his non-verbal behaviour runs a parallel course: when he asks, he kneels before Jim with his head bent to the left, when he asserts he looks straight at him and his sentences are less drawn-out, and when he demands he reaches for the fire-engine. Neither has any intention of giving up.

Otto once again: 'Me too, one go, meeee one go, meee too, just one...'. Jim does little more than crawl away and look behind him, angry just this once. Meanwhile, still crawling round ('Can I have a go, can I have a go, can I have a go?') they end up in the vicinity of the teacher, who sees that Jim is holding the fire-engine above his head. 'What is it, Jim?' she asks. 'I want to have the fire-engine,' he replies. 'You want to play with the fire-engine? But Otto finds it so beautiful he wants to play with it too. Can't Otto play with it? Otto knows it's yours and he'll give it back straight away.' She has hardly finished speaking but Jim already hands the fire-engine over to Otto. He explains what button to press for the siren; and so under the teacher's watchful eye Otto at last has his turn with the fire-engine. The teacher walks away and then turns round. As soon as she says that Jim can have it again, Otto gives it back. And so all ends well.

Jim and Otto are extraordinarily resolute: Jim because he resists Otto so long without defending himself physically and Otto for his persistence. This conflict also lasts for a relatively long time: 10 minutes. The average duration of a conflict between such young children is 18 seconds! They both persist because they manage to maintain the peace. Jim tolerates the older Otto and Otto knows how, after brief, impulsive grabbing movements, he has to restore the relationship with various placatory gestures. Another exceptional aspect of this incident is the trust that the teacher feels able to give them, as a result of which they immediately give up their resistance and come to meet each other half-way!

- Sometimes children themselves do not resolve their disagreements, as in the case of Otto and Jim. Then you need to mediate. Ask each in turn what they want.
  Repeat what the children have said and then ask: 'How are we going to resolve this?' The children themselves often come up with solutions; if not, put forward your own proposal and reassure the one who has to concede.

- When you have to sort out a conflict, your mediation should take into consideration the needs of both children. They have their own logic and, for that reason, quite often each is right in his own way.

18 Directing, exploring, conceding and conciliating

During a conflict, children use various ways of trying to assert their right. They can assertively direct, or gauge what the other wants and try out conciliatory ways of gaining what they want. Children can of course also choose to concede. By means of a concrete action, children often convey a relational message as well as the literal meaning of the verbal message. For example, a child can say that another child must keep away from his or her tower (verbal message) and at the same time, through an angry tone of voice, give a non-verbal, negative relational message (I don't like you, I'm not afraid of you, watch out!).

Directive or coercive actions

The child tries to impose his or her will on the other or get the other to do what he or she wants. Young children almost invariably do this in a negative fashion.
Some examples:
- grabbing a toy – Otto crawls after Jim and after a brief pursuit tries to snatch the fire-engine out of Jim's hands.
- looking angry – Bojan looks angrily at Jensely and Jensely slinks away.
- hitting, kicking and pushing – Megan draws back her arm and hits Samuel very hard on the head with the telephone.
- loud crying and fetching the teacher – Samuel runs to the teacher crying loudly and points at Megan.
- teasing – 'You're a monster!' says Maik.
- protesting – 'No,' replies Jim and holds the fire-engine behind his back.
- saying what you do or don't want – 'Give it to me,' says Fatima.
- giving arguments or explanations, as a rule to strengthen the one's own position – 'I had it first,' says Jeroen and holds tightly on to the doll that Lily wants to pull out of his hands.
- saying what the other must do – When Jim is waylaid by Otto, another child says: 'Then you must say "Don't do that Otto"'.

Exploratory probing

The child seeks to find out what the other child is doing or wants. The following are examples of this:
- seeking eye contact – He bends a little further forward and looks at Jim questioningly.

- indicating something – Bojan points at the train with an inquiring look.
- circling round a child – Urjandric walks up to Ozge and looks with interest at her game to see how he too might be able to join in.
- putting a question – Otto: 'I can, I can, can I have a go? Just one go?'

Soothing and conciliating

The child does something to meet the other half-way or to find a joint solution. He or she tries to restore the balance between giving and taking and taking turns (according to the rules of reciprocity). These are some examples:
- simply walking away – Samuel just walks away from the table in order to make another attempt to get hold of the bag a minute later.
- offering a toy – Urjandric picks up a doll and puts it down in front of Ozge.
- being affectionate – 'One go!' and Otto strokes Jim's cheek.
- homour or making a game of it – 'Get him, get him!' laughs Richella and thereby changes the conflict into a game.
- making a proposal – 'I'm a fireman too. Can we be two firemen?'
- reaching a compromise – 'I iron first, then you, OK?'

Conceding or losing

The child admits defeat, or can do nothing other than accept the role of the loser:
- concurring – 'OK,' sighs Charilain: 'I'll wait.' Charilain flops down and lets Nora iron the trousers.
- conceding (giving in) – Jensely walks away from the table and goes to play somewhere else.
- losing – Arjen stays sitting in the corner, sobbing.

In the following examples one sees how children are reconciled after a brief clash, either by a thoughtful act (Prosper, in the first example), or offering something (Timo, in the second example), and so, by following the rule of reciprocity, restoring the balance.

Nischa wants to get Jessica's orange | Jessica runs away with the orange and gives a challenging look to Nischa and Richella | Then it became a game

Restoring the balance

Prosper (3;4) and Aisha (3;1) are playing at the table with farm animals. As part of their play, Prosper strikes with his animal at Aisha's animal, but in doing so he hits Aisha's hand, making Aisha cry. Prosper is at once sorry. He looks sympathetically at Aisha, open-mouthed. While still crying, Aisha then hits Prosper gently in the face. They both turn round to see if there is a teacher anywhere near. Prosper shows he understands that she has been hurt: 'ow, ow,' he says, 'ow, with the pig?' Aisha nods. 'Ow, with the pig?' asks Prosper again, 'yes?' Aisha shakes her head, still crying. 'What then?' he asks. 'You,' cries Aisha and points with her animal at Prosper. He grabs his own hand and asks: 'Here, here?' Aisha nods, putting her hand in her mouth to soothe the pain. 'From mine here, knocked your hand,' declares Prosper and shows his own hand to Aisha. Aisha does not respond to this and the children go on playing together with their animals as before.

Timo (3;6) and Sylvano (3;6) are playing together in the building corner. Timo tries to take the blocks from Sylvano. He pulls the block towards him, out of Sylvano's hands and says: 'I like you, I like you. That alright?' 'No, that's not right,' says Sylvano, but he lets go of the block. Timo immediately says: 'I get a new one for you,' and walks away with the block. 'I get a new one. And you one too, heh?' Sylvano goes on playing with another block lying in front of him. Timo walks toward several blocks. 'I got it!' He shouts, 'I got it! Look!' He picks up a new block and gives it to Sylvano. Sylvano turns round smiling and takes the block: 'A new one, thank you.' Timo goes and sits on the ground by the blocks and the children play on together.

How often do they do it?

When children want something from the other, or if they specifically don't want something, in 91 percent of clashes they employ one or other form of coercive action. Two- and three-year-olds still often do this by physical means: in 42 percent of their clashes they shove, hit or kick, or snatch a toy. Children can also make their displeasure or anger very clear by walking off with the toy, by putting on an angry face or pointing accusatively. We en-

I like you

Making it good: I've made a new one, have you too?

countered this, at least once, in 59 percent of all clashes. In 69 percent of clashes, children express verbally what they do or do not want, but they still use arguments much less often: only in 24 percent of the clashes were arguments heard. Both from our research and the work of others it is evident that physical means (hitting, kicking) declines and the use of verbal resources (explanation, giving arguments, offering suggestions) increases from the third or fourth year.

In more than half (57 percent) of the clashes, it is found that the children explore what the other is doing or wants. They do this by pointing at something or looking questioningly, or, if they want to play together, by lingering round the other and explicitly watching what they are doing. Trying to establish eye-contact is another way. We found that two- and three-year-olds do not put questions to each other - only in 19 percent of all their clashes. Some children also have propitiatory, conciliatory manners in their repertoire, but again these are less often seen. Soothing acts and remarks occurred in 18 percent of conflicts. In only 11 percent of clashes did children make conciliatory gestures by laughing or smiling at the other, by stroking or giving a kiss. In 5 percent of clashes, children said something kind to propitiate the other.

Lessons in psychology

In chapter 5 we described the way babies playing together take their first steps toward understanding each other's emotions and thoughts. By the end of their first year they already realise that they can influence the other by their non-verbal utterances and first 'words'. (Doherty-Sneddon, 2003). However, they still have to learn that if they want to get their way and also want to remain friends they must first think what it is the other wants or thinks. If, for example, they see a very attractive object they forget that the other child is playing with it and wants to continue playing. Conflicts contribute to the acquisition of this insight. They discover through such clashes that the other too has (other) desires and thoughts (Piaget, 1967; Killen & Nucci, 1995; Killen & De Waal, 2000). One can see how far they are able to take this into account and adapt their behaviour accordingly in the strategies that children apply in order to stay together.

Two-year-olds already do this, often non-verbally, but three-year-olds are much more able to use language (De Haan & Singer, 2003). When they clash, they give more explanation, more frequently give reasons why they want something. They more often make a suggestion or agree a compromise that involves themselves giving up something.

Pedagogical tips to remember

Observe what kinds of action a child uses during a clash with another child: directive/coercive, exploratory, propitiatory/conciliatory. If the opportunity arises, try to extend the child's repertoire.

19 The third child: the spectator

When two children clash, there are often other children nearby. What does the third child do? Does he or she get involved or not?

The taking-it-in gaze

Jan (3;11) is building with blocks on the ground. Jeroen (3;5) is playing next to him with plastic farm animals. There are a great many toys lying all round both boys. Onno (2;6) toddles up, sees a goat, picks it up and quickly goes off with it. Jan rushes after Onno and tries to pull the goat out of his hand. Jeroen watches the wrestling wide-eyed. When Jan returns with the goat he goes on with his play.

Chasing away together

Nora (3;1) approaches Tayrell (2;11) and Jerzy (3;3) who are sitting together on the sofa with a magazine. Jerzy is playing with a pair of sunglasses in his hand and doesn't see Nora coming, but Tayrell does and kicks his feet in her direction. Nora goes and sits on a chair and looks uneasy. Tayrell kicks twice in the air in her direction and then waves his arm with a hitting motion. Jerzy sees this gesture by Tayrell and imitates it. The two boys imitate each other a few times with these movements and then Tayrell begins to shout at Nora 'Go away, Donnadonna' and looks at Jerzy, who in turn imitates him. This continues until Jerzy points in the journal and the attention of the two boys' is distracted from the conflict. Nora then walks away.

Taking-it-in: what's happening there?   Tyrell begins, Go away!   Jerzy joins in, Go away, you!

Quintly (3;11), Bojan (3;9) and Vivianne (2;7) go to play in the sandpit. Bojan takes a shovel from the sandpit but Quintly snatches it from his hands. Vivianne looks to the camerawoman for help. Bojan and Quintly fight over the shovel. Vivianne looks constantly from one to the other. She herself is holding two shovels and she now looks at them. Then she turns to Bojan and offers him one of her shovels. But Bojan doesn't want this shovel, and just stands there looking angry and rather sorry for himself. Bojan becomes distracted and the conflict is over.

Doing nothing or joining in, but rarely mediating

As already remarked, when children clash there are often other children in the vicinity. Yet rarely will a third child get involved in a clash between two other children. In 70 percent of cases the other children do nothing (Van Hoogdalem, Singer, Sterck & Bekkema, 2005). They either pay no attention or they watch intently what is happening and round about them. The by-standers also cast frequent questioning looks toward the teacher, or look around searching for her. In our research, the children also often looked to the camerawoman for support. If they do anything further, as a rule they give their support to one of the two children, whom they assist by imitating, by hitting or shouting that something is not allowed, as when Jerzy joins Tayrell to chase off Nora. In rare cases, a third child will mediate, as in the last example where Vivianne offers her shovel; but this occurred in only 3 percent of the clashes when there were other children in the vicinity. Why is it that children so rarely intervene in the clashes of others? The simplest answer would be that they just don't notice these clashes: they happen too fast and are so quickly over. But that is not the whole story. Very often, we see children watching and doing nothing. Why is that?

In all probability, these children do nothing for the following reasons:
- Young children are totally absorbed in their gaze. What they see keeps them so busy they cannot at the same time reflect on what they make of it; all they can do is look intently in order to grasp what is going on.

Imitation: go away Donnadonna

Go away, Donnadonna

- Young children are still unable to see an event from more than one side. They are not yet cognitively equipped for this. But that is precisely what is needed if they are to mediate: to be able to see from different viewpoints. What does the one child want, what does the other want? How can I help both children? This cognitive limitation can also explain why, when young children do intervene, they choose the side of one of the two contestants. They often imitate the behaviour of the child they support. For this, they need only to look at the clash from the one viewpoint and side with that antagonist.
- Young children expect the teacher to help when it's necessary. They don't see it as their own job to intervene. One sees their reliance on the teacher in their behaviour: the third child often looks around as though thinking: does the teacher see this? What will she think of it? And if the teacher does nothing, then perhaps it's not all that serious. They look questioningly to the teacher instead of doing something themselves.

Pedagogical tips to remember

- Don't forget the children who witness rows of long-lasting disagreements! It is evident from the intent way they look on that they are very interested. Moreover, they are often horrified when physical blows are exchanged. They too need calming and comforting.

- Try to get them involved in talking about what has happened and about the reconciliation. Make it clear to them what the one wants or feels as well as the other.

Part 4

LEARNING MOMENTS

20 Clashes are opportunities to get to know the rules and opinions of others

According to the developmental psychologist Piaget (1967), it is through clashes that children learn that other children or adults have different opinions and desires. They learn that the world is constituted differently from what they had thought. This is the motor that drives the acquisition of new insights and enables them to overcome their own egocentrism – thinking that the other thinks as you do. Without such clashes with others, there can be no cognitive or moral development (Killen & De Waal, 2000). The kind of rules and other opinions that children learn through clashes becomes clear when we look at the content of their clashes. Two- and three-year-old children in child day-care centres are found to clash mainly over the following issues:

- *The 'keep-away-from-me' feeling* – children have to learn to respect each other's boundaries. They have to learn to touch each other gently. There is a boundary between wrestling or romping around and really hurting each other. Children must learn to keep away and leave the other child alone if he or she wants to be left in peace and quiet. The rules are thus: 'don't hurt each other' and 'don't disturb each other.'
- *Clashes over objects* – children have to learn to share toys and to accept that another child may play with something that he or she has enjoyed having. The rules are: 'take your turn'; 'share together'; 'Whoever has something can keep it'. The fact that something looks attractive does not mean that you can have it. Young children have to learn to control impulsive behaviour; this is an important social skill.
- *The 'I-want-to-join-in-too' fuss* – children have to learn social skills if they are to enhance their chances of being allowed into the games of other children. However, they also have to learn that children sometimes don't want to admit newcomers, they want to continue playing undisturbed.
- *Clashes over ideas about play* – when children play together it is inevitable that now and again there will be disagreements. One child wants to build a tower as high as possible, the other finds that knocking it down is the real pleasure. Two children want to play 'mother' but neither wants to be 'baby'. Children have to learn to negotiate, to give and take, if they are to be able to go on playing together.

Quite often, several issues all play a role at once in a clash between children. One child picks up a piece of a puzzle that another child is playing with, leading to a 'thing clash', but subsequently it turns out that the child wanted to join in and so it also becomes an 'I-want-to-join-in-too' hullabaloo.

We found in our research that most clashes had to do with a 'keep-away-from-me' feeling and having, or wanting to have things (see table). These two issues each accounted for almost fifty percent of all conflicts. Clashes over different ideas about play were less frequent, although the number increased with older children, whose play increasingly follows plans that they invent together.

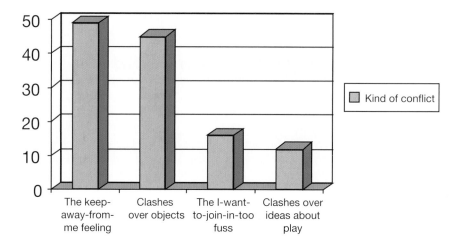

Reason for clash in percentages of all clashes. Frequently there was more than one reason for the clash operating at the same time.

21 The keep-away-from-me feeling

Clashes that arise from the 'keep-away-from-me' feeling in fact give the child the opportunity to take in some very basic moral principles:

Rule: You must not hurt the other and you must not ruin his or her things or constructions. This is a cardinal moral rule.

Rule: You should leave the other in peace if that's what he or she wants. Having respect for another's privacy means that you let the other determine how close you may come. Children must learn to respect both the psychological room and the physical territory of others.

Hurting each other

Jan (3;11) and Marja (3;6) are playing beside each other in the sandpit. Jan is playing with sand moulds and Marja is digging a hole. Jan's mould rolls into Marja's hole and he wants to get it out. Marja's trowel hits Jan's arm – whether accidentally or on purpose is not clear, but Jan is cross and tries to take the trowel away from Marja. Marja won't have this and gives Jan a hard blow with the trowel across his arms.

Knocking down towers

Raouf walks up to the building corner where Sylvano is building a splendid, tall tower from blocks. 'What are you making?' asks Raouf. 'This is a chimney', explains Sylvano. Raouf picks up two blocks from the ground, makes a strange noise and lays the blocks on top of the tower. 'Aaawiii', he then screams, seizes the tower and pushes it over, all the while watching Sylvano mischievously. Appalled, Sylvano sees

Aawieeee, Raouf knocks the tower over

Jody points: he spoiled it

97

his splendid tower collapse. He at once makes his way to the teacher to tell her his complaint, with Jordy coming to back him up.

Pointing at Raouf he says: 'He knocked it down.' Raouf looks down guiltily. From a distance, the teacher tells him he mustn't do that; Sylvano and Jordy return to their play and ignore Raouf, who then walks away.

The principle moral rules

Rule: You must not hurt the other.

Maintaining this moral rule is one of the teacher's main tasks. She has to ensure, after all, that the group is a nice, safe place for every child. So we don't hurt each other by pushing, hitting, kicking, pulling or biting. Research shows that most children from a very young age look afraid or aghast when they hurt someone or destroy something, or if another child does it. There seems to be a natural elementary moral (Killen & De Waal, 2000), but if this so, such an awareness has to be further developed, and this requires education. Here too nature seems to assist: children are often uncertain or anxious when they feel they are about to go too far. At such moments, they cast a questioning look toward the teacher or into the camera. If the teacher or another adult does not react, the children think that it's OK and this can lead to an exaggeration of the naughty behaviour. We saw this in the sand-throwing example in Chapter 8: when the camerawoman did not react the children became wilder. The example of Jan and Marja in the sandpit demonstrates how children can also think that they are fully entitled to hit the other. Marja probably thinks that Jan is beginning to pester her. Perhaps Jan thinks that Marja is beginning. In a case like this the teacher can ask both children what they think how they feel about the situation. She can then emphasise that both children were hurting each other. Is that nice? Are we happy about that? What was our rule? Don't hurt each other! Who can think of a plan to make it up again?

Raouf looks down guiltily

Raouf walks away

Rule: You should leave the other in peace if that's what he or she wants.

In a group of fourteen young children, it is impossible to prevent them absolutely from getting in each other's way, but with many clashes a red light should start flashing in front of the teacher. Are there places where children can play undisturbed? Is there a place for children to run, to romp and scream at the top of their voice? Is the material in the corner sufficiently challenging? Are some children bored? Young children sometimes would like the attention of older children, but these are not always very keen on it; in which case, it can be a good idea to give these older children the chance to play at their own higher level without being harassed by the little ones. At other times both the older and younger children have much to offer when they all play together.

The rule of leaving each other in peace is one that children have to learn in practice. It's about respecting the individual right to something for yourself, without others. It is precisely through minor clashes that children learn what they can and what they shouldn't do, for this rule is essentially about feeling and intuition: sometimes the other child enjoys contact and at other times not. Moreover: what one child likes, another child may find extremely irritating. Children have to learn to be sensitive to negative signals from the other and in such a case to stop. The teacher doesn't have to be always interfering; as a rule it is sufficient if she herself sets a good example in her dealings with the children. Perhaps now and again she can refer to the rule ('Now then, leave Sylvano in peace!'). Or she can perhaps further explain why he should be left in peace: he is playing happily on his own and wants to build as tall a tower as possible. Only when a child is often felt by his or her peers to be a nuisance is extra pedagogical attention needed.

'Don't hurt each other' may be a more straightforward rule than 'leave each other in peace', but it is a rule that is learned much more through trying it out: children learn the boundary between romping and fighting through practice. Knocking down each other's tower is sometimes taken as mere play. This was probably Raouf's intention, but he had failed to grasp the signals given by Sylvano and Jordy, who reacted to his destruction of their work as an aggressive act and therefore wrong.

Children learn the rules by determining among each other the boundaries between what is alright and what is not. With each new concrete situation they have to find out for themselves how to apply the rules, even when these rules have been explained, imposed and supervised by adults.

Pedagogical tips to remember

- Set a good example yourself by respecting the psychological space of the children and by not screaming or grabbing children roughly.

- Help children to get a feeling for the rules by talking with them about what they feel and what they want; and allow them the room to learn them through practice.

- Always intervene when children hurt each other: explain the rule, comfort and conciliate.

22 Clashes over objects

Clashes over objects occur very frequently with young children. Whereas avoiding clashes related to that 'keep-away-from-me' feeling is mainly a matter of developing a sense of the physical and psychological boundaries of others, in the case of clashes over objects it is a question of learning rules concerning ownership.

Who is allowed to play with the lady's bag

Samuel (2;3) approaches and takes from the table the lady's bag from which Megan (2;9) has been inseparable the whole day. Megan starts, says 'No!' and tries to pull the bag out of Samuel's hands. Samuel won't let go, he looks frustrated, and the two children wrestle for possession. Megan has a telephone in her hand and hits Samuel's hand with it, but Samuel, grim-faced, holds on the bag. Megan then raises her arm and gives him a hefty blow to the head with the telephone. That hurt! Samuel holds his head and runs crying to the teacher. Megan looks guiltily around her.

Catch me if you can!

Jessica (3;1) is wandering around. Then she walks up to Nischa (3;8), grabs a plastic orange out of her hand and walks away with it. Nischa tries to get the orange back, but Jessica is already skipping away laughing. 'No!' says Nischa and runs after Jessica. After one turn round the table Nischa manages to grab Jessica and tries to wrestle the orange out of her grasp. Jessica won't give in. She escapes and runs to the

Samuel grabs the lady's bag

The children wrestle for possession

kitchen holding the orange tightly to her. Now Yassir (3;0) and Richella (3;7) also try to get hold of the orange. Jessica looks challengingly at the children as she once more runs away round the table. 'Get her, get her!' laughs Richella and the three children run after each other, with Jessica alternately running and then waiting, daring them, while the three pursuers try to catch her.

An attractive object in the hands of another child becomes twice as attractive

An experiment: while you are talking with a colleague, suddenly and explicitly glance to your left, and the chances are that your colleague will immediately look that way too. This is reflex behaviour shared by children and adults alike. People tend to look toward whatever has caught the attention of others. Behavioural scientists believe this sort of behaviour has survival value. If someone suddenly looks somewhere, it could signal danger! If someone looks intently in a certain direction, it must surely be very interesting or tasty, to which a natural reaction seems to be: 'I want that too!' Such innate mechanisms probably play a role in children's preference for the toys of others. A plaything become more attractive if another child is playing with it, and so you try to play with it too! We see this happen so often in day-care centres. But the other won't so easily let the object go. What you've got you want to hang on to! This too seems to be an innate reaction. If they have something nice or something delicious, children will happily show it to others or even share it, but letting them take it is an entirely different matter. Finally, the law of the strongest plays a major role in such clashes. Young children very quickly grasp that if the teacher is not looking they can take something away from weaker children and go unpunished.

In the childcare centre we see that teachers always maintain two rules:

1. Rule: you must not take something from someone if they are playing with it, even if you are stronger.
2. Rule: you must play together with toys that are scarce; either by playing together or by taking turns to play. Because all children have the same right, they must learn to apply the rule of reciprocity.

Megan hits Samuel hard with the telephone

Samuel runs crying to the teacher

It depends on the teacher's values and norms where she lays the emphasis, whether on sharing together or on respect for individual possession. Both rules apply in most child centres and are applied according to the actual situation. There are also cultural differences relevant to this point: from our interviews with mothers, it seems that Dutch mothers emphasise more the right to possession (the individual right) while Moroccan mothers place more emphasis on sharing.

In practice, teachers are not always consistent, partly because it is not always clear which rule should be applied. For example, if we take the clash between Samuel and Megan over the lady's bag, Megan has probably played with the bag for quite a while, but when Samuel grabs it, she is not actually playing with it. Can she still legitimately claim ownership? Also, children themselves make their rules for what is and what is not permissible, and sometimes they can change the situation during the clash. Thus, in the second example, the quarrel is resolved by the children themselves converting the original affront, the seizure of the orange, into a game of 'catch me if you can!'

Pedagogical tips to remember

- Discuss clearly with your colleagues and with parents what it is that you more especially want the children to learn: sharing attractive toys together or the right to individual possession and use

- Use clashes as opportunities to teach them a positive moral principle of giving and taking.

- Resist the temptation always to resolve clashes over objects by buying more of the same.

- Teach children the take-your-turn rule.

23 The I-want-to-join-in fuss

During free play time, children often walk around looking for playmates or an interesting activity going on somewhere. If they see something that attracts them, the trick is then to find a way of joining in. Sometimes this is effortless, but often there is resistance. If a clash ensues but the child really wants to join in, it's down to the art of persuasion, or seduction, to get oneself accepted. In this kind of clash, it's not so much a question of learning social rules but more of still having to master the right social skills.

I can do it too, look!

Rahul (3;8) and Daan (3;10) are playing with a train on the floor. Walid (3;8) wants to join in with them, so he squats down near the boys and picks up a wagon that he wants to hook on to the train. Daan looks distrustfully at him and says: 'Balid, Balid!' 'Balid's not my name!' says an irritated Walid. 'But you mustn't do it like that!' observes Daan, referring to the wagon Walid wants to couple. 'It can go like that, can't it? Walid turns to Rahul, attempting to draw him into the discussion. Rahul says 'no', and turns away from Walid. It seems that the boys don't really want a new playmate. Walid sees that he must try a different approach. He tosses one of the wagons in the air: 'This, this, this is good, heh?' and looks at the boys laughing. Daan is still displeased, saying that the wagon is his, but then Walid shows them what you can do with a wagon: 'It can go in the house, look, it can go inside.' 'Oh, yes, that's funny' says Daan: 'Do that, Balid, put it down here.' The boys then play on as a threesome.

Walid wants to join in

The boys reject Walid

Walid attracts attention: look what I've got!

I want to play with the dolls with you

Urjandric (2;7) watches Ozge (3;8) playing with the dolls and wants to join in.
He walks toward one of her dolls and pulls the little blanket off, calling 'The baby! the baby!' whilst looking at Ozge. Ozge shouts angrily 'No, no, it's my baby!' and pick up the blanket from the ground. Urjandric walks away before stopping at a distance to watch Ozge. She is not entirely confident and shouts again, 'My baby, it's my baby!' and looks back at him crossly.' Urjandric turns this way and that, laughing playfully. He picks up a blanket from the ground, skips away with it and says: 'Mine, mine.' Ozge, irritated, tries in vain to get the blanket back again. Then the playful Urjandric tries another tack. He picks up another doll from the ground and lays it down in front of Ozge, saying to her: I want to do that with you too. But he has already got on the wrong side of Ozge and she'll have none of it: 'No, no, I don't want it , I got a baby already', and she throws away the doll that Urjandric has just presented. Urjandric slinks away.

Try to imitate and not be conspicuous

With young children, playing together is still a fragile enterprise, and a new-comer can easily disturb it. There is therefore a genuine interest in keeping other children out. There are also always children on the lookout for something new, whose interest is in being allowed to join in. Research suggests that about half the attempts made by children to join the play of others fail, and only rarely are they accepted at their first try. As a rule, they are only allowed to join in after one or two refusals. What can young children do to improve their chances of joining in?

Rule: first watch and understand what the others are doing. Children often just saunter round the other children and look inquiringly or ask if they can play too. This sort of behaviour does not impress the children with whom they would like to play and is usually brushed aside. Watching well and un-

Samuel wants to climb on the seesaw with Megan

Looking to the teacher: is this allowed?

derstanding what's going on is the indispensable preparation for the next step.

Rule: Do exactly what the other children are doing. Don't be conspicuous and don't interrupt their play. Giving the children an object that fits into their play can also help you gain admission. As we saw earlier, imitation is a powerful means of evoking a sense of togetherness.

If the child impulsively wants to reshape the pattern of play after his own idea – as Urjandric does in the example above – the chances are that he will be rejected. At first, Walid was also rejected because of his own initiative, but he managed to bring the other children round. He first makes it clear that he obeys them and stops when the other boys want him to. He makes positive contact by laughing and is in fact fortunate that his idea of what to do with the wagon meets with their approval.

Pedagogical tips to remember

- Take the rejected child and together watch the other children; talk about what they are doing. Try to soothe the child and to rein in his (or her) impulsiveness.

- Play with the child yourself, invite other children to play as well and through playing encourage the contact between the children.

- If the rejected child is different from the other children and if this is difficult to change, try to get the other children to have more understanding for being different. You can read more on this in the chapter on dealing with diversity.

- Be absolutely clear on the rules that hold for the group:
  the right of all children to play together;
  the right of a small group or an individual child to shut themselves off from others.

Megan has the whip-hand - she drags Samuel off the seesaw

Samuel looks peeved and slinks away

24 Clashing ideas over play

When playing together, children often quarrel over their ideas about how to play. Their ideas on the content of the play can sometimes differ - for example, when building, over how to build a house out of lego; or when dressing up, over a cap that sits wrongly; or in romping about together, over whether you should attack. With this sort of clash, one is dealing with important matters in children's lives: construction, clothes, aggression in play. In let's-pretend games too, children often have very different ideas. In this kind of game they create their own world and are strongly emotionally involved in it. There often arise minor conflicts, for instance over who should be mother and who baby, or over the events in a story. Such minor conflicts are usually a form of proto-negotiation. With each turn, they adopt a position: can they agree with the other, or do they still think it should be done differently?

On a journey

Suzanne (3;4) and Sarah-Noor (3;4) are in the house corner playing that they are off on a journey:
Sarah-Noor: 'We're in an aeroplane, aren't we?'
Suzanne: 'Yes.'
Sarah-Noor: 'We're almost there, you know.'
Suzanne: 'We're almost there.'
Sarah-Noor: 'We're still in Asia or somewhere.'
Suzanne: 'Yes, we're still in Asia.'
Sarah-Noor: 'We're not there yet. We're not there yet. When we're near the sky, we're there.'

Travelling with babies and bags

We're off!

Suzanne: 'Yes, when we're near the sky, we're there. But not where we are now. We're not there yet. Oh, we're almost there.'
Sarah-Noor: 'Yes, we're almost there.'
Suzanne: 'We're almost there. We almost have to get out. We have to get out. We must get out now.'
After having put some things in the bags, Sarah-Noor calls: 'We're there!'
Suzanne: 'No, we're not there yet. We're going toooooooot up again. We're not there yet, are we?'
Sarah-Noor: 'We're nearly there.'
Suzanne: 'We're nearly there.'
Sarah-Noor: Are we there yet?
Suzanne: 'No, we're not there yet. Almost. We're there. We're there again already.'
After some time, putting all the things in bags and taking them out again, putting babies in and out of carrycots, in and out of pushchairs, Suzanne calls 'Off we go!'

Sarah-Noor and Suzanne try out a number of techniques to convince the other of their own idea and at the same time to ensure that the relationship between them is not spoiled. These are very subtle adaptations of each to the other in which Suzanne generally takes the lead and Sarah-Noor is content to follow. Sarah-Noor does try to influence the course of the game but in words that muffle any suggestion of contradicting her friend: 'We're almost there, you know' and 'We're in Asia or somewhere.' She then dares make an assertion: 'When we're near the sky then we're there.' But Suzanne makes it clear that she's not yet ready for this: 'But not as we are now'. When Suzanne has decided it's time to leave the plane and Sarah-Noor confirms it (We're there!'), Suzanne changes her mind and emphasizes her move with a drawn out 'We're going toooooooot up again,' only to realise subsequently that this was rather brusque of her, and so she asks for assent to this turn: 'We're not there yet, are we?' Sarah-Noor concurs ('We're nearly there') and Suzanne acknowledges that Sarah-Noor is quite right: 'We're nearly there.' After a hopeful 'Are we there yet?' from Sarah-Noor, Suzanne asserts her position as leader once more with 'No, we're not there yet', but she ad-

We're going in the lift

Yeeeea.., I can push the button

mits, 'nearly' in order to be able to determine herself the exact moment of arrival.

In their 'let's-pretend' games children also put forward arguments and explanations for over-riding the other:

> Cas (3;7) (in the front seat of the tandem): 'Where do you want to go?'
> Vera (3;11) (behind):'To Germany.'
> Cas: 'That's too far.'
> Vera: 'But you can with the aeroplane, first with the bicycle and then ride to the aeroplane field.'
> Cas: 'Yes but that's too far as well.'
> Vera: 'Then with a taxi.'
> Cas: 'No this isn't a taxi.'
> Vera: 'With the ..with the?' …. but here her imagination seems to run dry.

In these negotiations over their play, children gain a great deal of experience with narrative. They negotiate with each other over the setting of the story. For instance:
• persons/animals – Nico: 'You're the doctor.' Emma: 'No, I'm ill.'
• place – Yves: 'You're in the prison.' Bob: 'No, this is a house.'
• props /attribution – Jon: 'This isn't a tart, it's a pancake.'
They also talk about what should happen and how it ends up, i.e. the plot:
Bart: 'We're going to do the washing up, yeh?' Mark: 'No.'
Through playing, and negotiating, they learn the basic narrative elements of which stories consist.

Stepping above yourself

In 'let's-pretend' games, where a child imagines something, he or she learns to think about their own everyday actions, gaining a certain distance, as it were, from what is seen and done every day by creating a representation of it. As Vygotsky puts it: "In play the child is always above his average age, above his daily behaviour" (1976, p. 552). In this sense, play creates what Vygotsky called a 'zone of proximal development'; that is, the child comes a step further forward and functions at a higher level during 'let's-pretend' games. In social 'let's-pretend' games where children negotiate with each other over roles and scripts, they create such a zone for each other: by articulating their imagined scenarios verbally, for each other, they stimulate each other to step out of the here-and-now and to reflect on different perspectives. Conflicts over the course and characteristics of the story are thus conducive to children's development. They learn to think about the logic of a story. This thinking and talking is a good preparation for later reading, where they will also have to use their imagination to picture the world described by a text. But children differ in the extent to which they play fantasy games, and also in the way in which they do it. In our research we compared the fantasy games of West Indian, Moroccan and Dutch children. We found no great differences between these groups in the amount of time they spent in fantasy play. In each group there were children who had absolutely no fantasy play at all. Some children played less often but longer. The games of the Dutch children more often consisted of multiple fantasized scenes enacted one after the other. They needed fewer concrete things to be able to play and more often thought about their roles and situations. They also talked more during their play. For example, they would not merely lick at a cornet-shaped duplo cone but would also say things like: 'Ooo, look, lovely ice-cream'; or give a verbal commentary on their story: 'My ambulance doesn't work. I'm going to make it.' Dutch children also negotiate more frequently than the others: 'This was our bed, wasn't it?'

Pedagogical tips to remember

Many conflicts are not about the playing itself, but about who is admitted to the game and who takes what role, over who can have certain playthings and so on. Sometimes, these minor conflicts prevent the children getting as far as actually playing. The teacher can help young children to create a good story together and talk about the story itself. In this way, they can suggest ideas that the children can then use in their own negotiations. She is an assistant in the collaborative act of thinking up a play script:

- Arrange an activity corner that will elicit a certain type of play.

- Make sure there are sufficient (but not too many) playthings to lend the story support and make the game involving for everybody.

- Take part in the game yourself, or discuss the roles in the script and make them all interesting.

- Give suggestions as to possible exciting events through which the children can see how important everyone's role in the game can be.

- If the game doesn't work out well – for instance, if problems of dominance arise between children – play with them in a subordinate role (a customer, the patient, the child).

Part 5

THE TEACHERS

25 The teacher: protector, authority and mediator

Young children are very good at handling clashes and sort out most of these conflicts without any need of help from teachers. Even after rows they often go on playing together. Nevertheless, teachers have a great influence – both indirectly, by supporting positive mutual relations between children, and directly, by intervening in clashes when necessary. We shall distinguish between three roles the teacher can play in these clashes between children:

1. The protector, who watches to see that all the children feel secure and maintain good, positive relations with each other.
2. The authority figure, who looks after values and norms, makes rules and agreements with the children and – when necessary – intervenes to remind them of these.
3. The mediator, who helps the children to find solutions together, re-connects and reconciles and in general encourages the development of social skills.

The protector

The more positive the mutual relations between children, the more open they are to finding solutions and reconciliation together. One of the teacher's main tasks is to ensure that children feel personally safe and recognized and function well in the secure context of the children's group. Teachers create a culture of tender affection. Parts 1 and 2 deal with what teachers can do to help generate a we-feeling between the children and how they can elicit, direct and support playing together. Teachers can in this way have an indirect influence on whether more or fewer clashes arise between children. In this regard, there are huge differences in the pedagogical approach of different teachers. In earlier research, we found in Finnish groups that two- and three-year-olds had on average 4 conflicts per hour (Singer & Hännikäinen, 2002). Compared with Dutch teachers, these Finnish teachers worked in a highly structured manner:

• The teachers organize the children's play activities for each day.
• During free play, the (on average) fourteen children were divided into two groups, each with a teacher. The teachers regularly played with the children.
• The play materials were carefully chosen in order to elicit particular activities from the children. Each day, something different was put in the most prominent place.

- The room was so divided that children had no need to disturb each other during play. The sleeping areas were also used to play in, with one group inside and the other out. As a result, the children had a large play space at their disposal.

An opposite situation was found in an Italian group investigated by one of our students. In this group 20 to 25 children played in a small space with minimal interference from the teacher. Children there had more than 30 conflicts per hour. Most Dutch groups adopt a middle position between the Finnish and Italian extremes – with an average 12 conflicts per hour. In our view, this is rather on the high side. There is considerable qualitative gain in adopting an active pedagogical policy to stimulate and support playing together. The higher the quality of the indirect pedagogical input, the more room the children will have to resolve their conflicts themselves and the less will be need for direct intervention by the teachers!

The authority figure

Of course, intervention is necessary now and again. Security also means being allowed to make mistakes, being allowed to be a small child and to experiment whilst knowing that someone is watching over you. You don't have to be able to do everything well because there is always someone there – the authority figure – who will see that everything is fine and stays fine. As the authority figure, the leader has the job of keeping a watch on boundaries, stopping children when they hurt each other, teaching them the rules and coming to agreements with the children. Children also need to be reminded of these rules and agreements sometimes, and to this end the direct intervention is an important way of helping children when clashes occur. It's sometimes necessary to explain the rule and talk over what it is that children want and feel.
This can be done in two entirely different ways that have very different effects on young children. The two approaches are discussed in 'Firmness with kid gloves '(chapter 26) and '(Unintentionally) unfair or angry' (chapter 27).

The mediator

When children cannot sort out a problem together, the solution is by no means always to be found in referring to a rule or agreement. In many situations it is wholly unclear what is fair, or what is the best solution. What is then required is to talk it over and to look for a solution together. Through such experience, children learn new social skills such as taking into account each other's feelings, talking instead of hitting and pushing, seeking compromise and reconciliation. Three chapters are devoted to mediation. Chapter 28 deals with the three-step procedure for teachers to take when mediating. Chapter 29 covers the way teachers can influence children's feelings and how they can help children to control violent feelings of rage, sorrow, disappointment and jealousy. Chapter 30 looks more deeply into the issue of talking – children talking and talking with children in order to resolve clashes.

Democracy for toddlers

Taken together, these three roles of the teacher have the aim of realising a pedagogical mission: 'democracy for toddlers'! Learning to resolve conflicts is part of learning to participate in the community and learning how to deal with opposite interests in a good way. This begins with toddlers. In a group with fourteen other toddlers there is constantly the potential for a clash of wants and needs and different opinions, whether it's a question of who can take possession of the fire-engine, who you can wrestle with and who not, or who can take part in a baking session. Moreover, in a group of toddlers some things are scarce and you have to learn to divide the cake fairly. Toddlers also learn to decide about such essential matters as whether to admit or exclude another from joining a game. It is also important for toddlers to learn to pay attention to others, to be able to see from the perspective of others, to deal with differences and to connect with others. In Part 3 we discussed the relational work and social skills of young children involved in clashes. Parts 2 and 4 looked at the many rules and customs that children have to grasp and learn to manipulate in order to belong to the group and play together. In this Part 5 it is the teachers who are in the spotlight: how can they help children play together and resolve conflicts through their direct involvement? Democracy at the toddler level is their mandate: it's the pedagogical task of teachers to get young children acquainted with this important principle, so very necessary for their life together.

Intermezzo: When do teachers intervene?

What do those teachers who were involved in our research do? Do they often intervene when children have conflicts? How do they intervene? We found that children mostly resolve their minor conflicts (mishaps) themselves. These usually pass over without the teacher even seeing them. With more significant disagreements teachers step in rather more often; and when it comes to full-blown rows the teachers usually intervene (see chapter 15 for the differences between these kinds of conflict). This is clearly seen in the percentages in the table below:

Table 3: Intervening in mishaps, disagreements and full-blown rows	
Kind of conflict	*Interventions by the teacher*
Mishap	12 %
Disagreement	19 %
Row	74 %

Apparently teachers give the children considerable room to sort out their differences themselves as long as the conflict does not become too fierce. When this is the case, as it usually is when there's a row, they mainly take care to preserve security. The question is how they do this. How do teachers intervene? We draw a distinction between a directive approach, where the teacher as authority figure makes sure that the children stop quarrelling, and a mediating approach.

Table 4: Incidence of the ways of intervening	
Kind of intervention by teacher	*Incidence*
Directive (the teacher as authority figure))	Total: 54 % In an angry tone: 20 % In a friendly-neutral tone: 80 %

For the directive approach, we distinguish between directive intervention, where one makes oneself clear whilst talking in a normal or friendly tone – 'Firmness with kid gloves' – and more authoritarian directive intervention – being clear and angry (and perhaps unintentionally unfair). We shall look more closely at this in chapters 26 and 27, while in chapters 28, 29 and 30, we shall go more deeply into the question of mediation.

26 Firmness with kid gloves

Teachers can be highly directive and give a clear lead whilst at the same time being very friendly. They are often directive in a quiet way, using very few words. They clothe their directive message: they give explanations or with a friendly joke remind the children of the rule.

Clarity and firmness: no beating about the bush

- 'Coos?'
- 'Back'
- 'Don't snatch'
- 'Paul, I don't want to see that, do I!'
- 'Just get off the chair.'

Intervention without verbal fuss works very well when a child immediately understands – and therefore already knows – that his behaviour is out of order. Even a warning glance can then be sufficient. A glance or a single remark works as a signal for the child to stop behaving negatively particularly when the child knows that the teacher has confidence in him or her.

Intervention without too many words does not work, however, when a child is too emotionally involved in a conflict. With just a 'Coos?' the teacher simply passes over such an emotional problem and so nothing is resolved. In a situation like that, it's beyond the powers of young children to arrest or change their behaviour on their own.

Yenthel and Nicole have a row over a bag

Nicole shrieks and the teacher hears

Firmness with kid gloves

- 'Now then, my lad, don't do that; it hurts.'
- 'You musn't just grab things like that, heh? Look, he was sitting on it before you.'
- 'Wim, no biting, OK? What did we agree together? Heh? I don't want any more biting. Alright? Agreed? Give Suzanne a kiss.'

Clear messages can be conveyed more gently. With just a few more words the teacher can direct her charges in a way that re-connects rather than alienates them. What she says is not only given a positive meaning through the (friendly or questioning) tone in which she says it, the (quiet) level of her voice, her attitude and facial expression, but also through the use of various small words (for example, heh? OK? just, shall we?) or words that indicate that she likes the child ('now then, my young fellow, don't do that', 'what have you done, sweetheart?') and of course through non-verbal actions, such as putting an arm round a child or taking him or her on her lap. The kid gloves ensure that children are more receptive to whatever the teacher wants, with the effect that they are prepared to follow her.

Rules and agreements

When we look closely at the way teachers give direction, it seems that – consciously or unconsciously – they often appeal to rules. But to young children not all rules are equally clear. Teachers often say things like:
- Nobody's stupid.
- Each time it's somebody else's turn.
- Everyone can go up.
- Yes, we can always help each other, heh?
- All children are allowed in the cupboards.

From the use of words that refer to a general situation, one can infer in these examples that they each appeal to a rule that applies to the whole: nobody, everyone, each other, we, each time. They are not specific to any particular

The teacher asks: what's happened?

In a friendly voice the teacher makes clear to Yenthel the take-your-turn rule

time or place or child. This kind of word or sentence is a signal to the child that it's a question of a rule.

Children discover many rules for themselves without any need for discussion over them.

We saw this with Robert in chapter 11: Robert was new to the group and quickly grasped which rules he had to observe. Sometimes a rule is formulated as an agreement, as in the case of the biting Wim: 'Wim, no biting, OK? What did we agree together? Heh?' Ronald, the teacher reminds him of what he knows very well. This occurs more often: 'Yes, but if you put it down in the group, then everyone can play with it. That's what was agreed, otherwise you must put it away in the drawer.' Evidently, this teacher has at some time agreed the rule with the whole group. Now she is pointing to a specific situation, and she is giving the child her own responsibility – which is how rules often work: she is appealing to the child to contribute her bit to the common good of the group's life together. This should be enough to get rid of – or even prevent - a problem. But make sure that these really are agreements. Only too often it's a matter of a rule that has never been discussed!

Do-rules are more effective

It is important that teachers distinguish between 'do-rules' and 'don't-rules'. Don't-rules are rules like: don't sit in each other's way; don't sit on the other's work. Examples of do-rules are: take your turn; playing together is nicer; you can help if the other agrees. Do-rules are certainly more effective; they provide children with a way out of conflict. All the emotional energy that comes with conflict can be channelled in another direction. Don't-rules, on the other hand, merely tell children to stop their behaviour, and that can sometimes be very difficult.

Kinds of rules

In Part 4, when discussing learning moments, it became clear that more than one rule can apply in conflicts. When there is a clash over a toy, for example, the 'take your turn' rule might apply, but so also might the rule 'I

| Samuel takes the purple stamp | Megan takes it back again, Samuel is angry | The teacher: can he borrow the purple one, then you take the orange one instead |

was already playing with it, so keep off!' Children have to learn to get a feeling for, and to discover together which rule should apply in a particular situation. When a teacher responds in a directive fashion, it helps if she explains why she is doing this. Very often it's a question of rule.

To simplify the forest of rules, it can be helpful if teachers make distinctions for themselves between different kinds of rule. This can also help when explaining the rules to children. There are five kinds of rule that are always coming up in toddlers' playrooms and child day-care centres:
1. *Rules about reciprocity*: take your turn; give and take; if you've done something wrong, make it good; take it into account if another child is smaller or can do less.
   These rules mainly apply between children, but also in teacher-child relations: after all, teachers want to give the child as much room as they can. See chapters 2 and 3.
2. *Rules about equality*: All children are allowed to play with the bicycle; nobody is allowed to scream loudly; all children must help with the clearing up. These are rules which say that all children shall be treated the same.
3. *Rules about individual rights*: don't disturb; whoever is playing with a plaything can continue to play with it. Children often appeal to these rules to claim their own rights, something that teachers can support.
4. *Rules related to solidarity*: everybody belongs; we should play together; we can help each other. These are rules for fostering togetherness and responsibility for each other
5. *Rules for giving and accepting direction*. Of course, these rules apply in the first place to the relation between the teacher and children. The teacher is the authority figure who sees that everything runs well. The children must accept direction and be obedient when the teacher requests it. But the teacher must also ensure that she does not misuse her power by making children afraid of her, or by giving them absolutely no space. One can also speak of direction-giving and -accepting between the children themselves, and also of protest if one child assumes a superior position. If, for example one child masters a game better than the other, the teacher can say: 'Now, you must do exactly what Naomi says, Manja.'

Cardinal rules

Young children grow up in a forest of rules, so it is important that teachers should be clear about what are the principle or cardinal rules. Cardinal rules are those rules that hold always and everywhere. They are the rules for which the teacher stops everything in order to talk about them, the rules for which she finds it important to establish clear agreements. The rule 'do not hurt each other' is one such cardinal rule.

Beside this, teachers will have practical cardinal rules relating to safety, for example: football only in the playground; no throwing of blocks. And just as rules are most important, it is also important when exercising them to do so firmly, but with kid gloves:

- They provide structure and safety.
- They promote the cohesion of the group: these are 'our' rules.
- They allow children to grip on to something: they are tools children can use to control their own behaviour.
- They provide children with a context for the development of a sense of social responsibility.

Firmness with kid gloves gives to children their own worth, gives them the space to listen and gives them the words to think about.

Pedagogical tips to remember

- Preferably give do-rules.

- Make it clear to yourself what kind of rule you are setting and regularly run through the background of the rule: reciprocity, equality, individual rights, or solidarity.

- Make clear the distinction between cardinal rules (that should always be obeyed) and rules that you have to learn to get a feeling for, and over which you may have a different opinion as to whether they only apply in particular situations.

- Only intervene if you know for certain what is going on and adapt your solution to the children's logic.

27 Unintentionally unfair or angry

Taking a strong line and imposing solutions to conflicts on children has its risks. If the teacher doesn't know what has happened she can easily put the blame on the wrong child or impose a solution that is unacceptable to one of the two children. The teacher can show her disapproval so clearly that the child becomes totally confused and angrier rather than calmer. It regularly happens that a disagreement between children flares into a real row after the teacher has stepped in to intervene (Singer, 2002; Singer & Hännikäinen, 2002).

Not fair

Anja (3;5), Karin (3;2) and Willem (3;5) wander round the playroom looking for something to interest them. Anja sees a telephone and draws Karin's attention by calling her name. Willem also seems interested and rushes over to Anja and the telephone, faster than Karin. Willem grabs the telephone and Karin protests: 'Uhhhh, uhhhh.' Karin throws a questioning look toward the teacher, who reacts with a warning: 'Karin!' Willem hugs the telephone to himself and the two girls seem to give up. But a few seconds later a new clash flares up. Anja tries to seize the telephone back again. Willem screams in protest: 'Aauwwww!' Now Anja gets a warning from the teacher: 'Don't grab!' And she tells Willem that he must come and play with the telephone next to her. Willem begins to talk with mummy and daddy on the 'phone. The two girls walk away and Willem remains behind, on his own with the teacher.

Watch me!

Bobby (3;11), Theo (3;8), Aafke (3;2) and Maarten (3;10) are playing at the table with wooden blocks and sticks. They each have a wooden hammer. Bobby playfully begins to tap Aafke's head with his hammer. At first Aafke laughs at this and imitates Bobby, but then suddenly she gets a real crack on the head. She pulls an unhappy, frightened face and looks toward the teacher, who has seen exactly what happened and gives Bobby a warning: 'No hitting, Bobby!' For a while all goes well, but then Bobby gives Aafke another crack on the head. She starts crying. The teacher has had enough. First she consoles Aafke and then she grasps Bobby and says to him: 'Go and tell Aafke you won't do it again. That's really not nice, I don't like that, you hear me?' Bobby doesn't respond and looks away angrily. When this approach doesn't work the teacher pulls Bobby's face toward her so that he has to look at her. In an angry tone she says: 'You must listen to me, because I don't like that. You wouldn't like it if Aafke hit you.' Then she pushes him away from the table with the wooden blocks: 'Go and play somewhere else.' Bobby then wanders around with an angry-cum-sorrowful, dejected face and plays alone with the doll's house. When another child accidentally touches him he immediately gives them an angry push.

Behind the back

Branco (2;7) and Gianni (2;2) are both playing with blocks near the teacher. Gianni is busy taking blocks from one side of the group to the other. He quickly grabs one of Branco's blocks and craftily hides it behind his back. The teacher has seen nothing. Branco however has seen very well, and shouts 'Noooooo!' and tries to get the block back. Gianni swiftly moves away with the block, without the teacher being able to see him. The teacher sees that Branco is upset and consoles him by pointing out the blocks that he can take: 'Look, there are the blocks.' Afterwards, Branco looks at Gianni resentfully.

Unjustly accusing

Above all else, the teacher must avoid becoming party to the conflict herself. She does so when she doesn't know what has been going on and yet chooses the part of one child, as the teacher did in the example above by siding with Willem when, in fact, the girls had the telephone first. When a teacher takes the side of the culprit and accuses the victim, or if she imposes an unjust solution, she unintentionally boosts the power of the child she has unjustly vindicated. This child is now assured of the almighty teacher's support and has no need to concede his or her position. With an ally like that, you don't need to admit to anything or to negotiate. In this way children forget the

Gianni takes Branco's block and holds it behind his back

Gianni walks away with it. The teacher sees nothing

The teacher comforts him and points to other blocks

rules of reciprocity and the 'winner' then goes all out for his or her individual right.

When children feel unfairly treated by the teacher, this gives rise to very strong feelings, much more so than when a child is unfairly treated by another child. A child probably feels much more impotent and afraid in the face of an 'unfair' teacher than against another child. After all, the child expects protection and security from the teacher. On the one hand, we saw children who took revenge on their opponent after an unfair teacher intervention; on the other hand we saw children who knew how to use the teacher by immediately starting to cry. Almost invariably, an unfair intervention on the part of the teacher leads to children falling out with each other.

Openly becoming angry

Young children can of course make teachers angry. Children who just don't want to listen, who easily and often cry, scream, kick or bite can irritate teachers enormously and sometimes push them almost to desperation. But should you openly show this to young children? In our research we encountered teachers who, in an angry tone of voice, made such remarks as:
- 'Alright, Mr Squeaky, don't squeak all at once.'
- 'We don't squeeze, or I'll put you down in the kitchen.'
- 'Are you off again?'
- 'You always start.'
- 'Why do we have to shriek like that? (while the teacher pulls the child away roughly).'

Intervening in a cold, negative tone and with an angry face is found not to work well with young children. They don't listen and persist with their truculent behaviour, as in the above example of Bobby. In such situations, the teacher conveys a negative message over what the child is doing (a don't-rule), a negative relational message (I don't want to see you, I don't like you) and at the same time asserts her superior power (you will do what *I* want). This is probably too much for two- and three-year-olds; they get upset.
When children are tired or very wound up there is a much greater chance that rows and tears will follow. There is then too much emotional energy to express in playing together with other children. The tension is too much, the children become uncontrolled and any minor thing is enough to trigger anger or distress. If in such a situation the teacher is angry with a child who hits or kicks, matters only become worse. When the teacher only tells the child what is forbidden, what is the child to do with all the emotional energy that has brought him or her to the point of explosion? Moreover, an angry teacher cannot help a child to know his or her own feelings and seek other ways of dealing with them. It is probably much more effective simply to say that hurting each other is not allowed and then to console and calm all the children involved. If a teacher wants to show her anger, it's much better simply to look stern. The child sees that it has done something serious , but at

the same time that the teacher has her feelings under control. This is much less distressing. And if the teacher has indeed expressed her anger – which will of course happen occasionally – it is important to be reconciled with the child after a short interval. Give the child a hug or a caress and say you're friends again. If the teacher helps the child to defuse the excess of emotion and to channel the energy elsewhere, there is much less chance that the unacceptable behaviour will be repeated.

What should a teacher do with her anger?

Everyone is familiar with irritation and anger. The causes differ from person to person: the unreasonableness of the child who persists in demanding attention even when you have done your best; children who are constantly whining or starting rows with other children; a child who, after you have said a hundred times that something is not allowed, nevertheless goes ahead and does it again. But where one teacher gets worked up, another colleague may be able to take can this kind of provocation in her stride. Just occasionally do all the teachers find a particular child a trouble-maker; and then all the teachers and management have to be on their guard. Teachers often feel that such a child transgresses their boundaries in a way that they find wholly unacceptable. It then becomes a kind of adult conflict – 'The child has overstepped my boundaries and done something to me' – while the teachers have to continue providing the security that the child badly needs.

Pedagogical tips to remember

When you *are* angry:

- Face the fact squarely that you are angry and talk with your colleagues about it.
  If the feeling of anger is really acute, ask your colleague if she will take over responsibility for the child. When the anger passes off, try to understand what made you so angry.

- Force yourself to do something very different, for example, clear up the toys. Remind yourself that no emotion is permanent and that the emotion you now feel will gradually disappear if you are busy with something else elsewhere.

- It often helps if you can find positive things in the child. Compare your own observations with those of a colleague. Do you see any differences?

- Sometimes a child's behaviour can (unconsciously) remind you – say - of your younger brother who was always crying, or of a child that bullied you at school. Of course, such memories have nothing to do with the child in front of you, but they can certainly get in your way!

- If all your colleagues find the child a serious nuisance, seek help from outside the team, because without such outside help you are never going to overcome the problem.

Try to be fair:

Quite often the teacher only notices the clash once the children begin to make a noise, when they begin screaming or crying. She then has to get some idea very quickly of what's going on. The following tips can help:

- Quickly gauge what kind of conflict this is: a keep-away-from-me clash; a clash over things; an I-want-to-join-in-too hullabaloo; a clash of ideas or a combination of two or more of these types of clash.

- Quickly try to get an idea of what the one and the other want. Keep in mind that in this kind of clash both children may be right in their own way.

- If you don't clearly know what led up to the conflict, don't do anything and see what transpires further. Only intervene in directive fashion if a cardinal rule is at stake.

- Make it good afterwards if you find you have treated one child unfairly.

28 Mediating and connecting: the three R's

The teacher can also direct children by mediating, thus giving them the tools to handle their conflicts and reconcile themselves. How can she do this? How does it work?

What she has to set in motion is a three-step procedure and these steps should be learned and recalled whenever the occasion demands. The three steps – the 3 R's – that she has to learn to implement are:

- *recognition*: keeping eye and mind open to both sides of the situation. The teacher makes sure she has an eye open for what is actually taking place between the children, so that she can immediately connect with their logic. This is the step of *insight*.
- *resolution*: by thinking of solutions for the children's problem, the teacher gives them the means to control their behaviour and their emotions. This is the step of *good ideas*.
- *reconciliation*: the teacher puts her efforts into getting them to play together again. This is the step of *restored relations*.

Then you should say so

Anissa is brushing Bridget's hair, but Bridget is not enjoying it. She looks cross. The teacher asks: 'Don't you like that?' 'No' she answers and retreats into herself while Anissa continues brushing her hair. 'Then you should say so' says the teacher, and then to Bridget, 'Anissa doesn't like it.' Bridget turns round to Anissa, looks at her crossly and says 'Anissa, I don't like it.' Anissa stops.

Adam and Bill both want the doll.
Adam cries and the teacher consoles him

They both want the doll.
How are we going to resolve this?

Branco offers the doll

He wants to show you…

Megan (2;9) sits at a table writing with a felt-tip on a piece of paper. Samuel (2;3) comes up and taps on the paper to point out something. Megan protests and pushes Samuels hand away. The teacher sees it and says to Megan: 'He's only pointing.' Then she asks Samuel: 'What is it?' and to Megan the teacher says: 'He wants to show what he has at home,' and then, encouraging Samuel, 'Say it then. You must ask, heh Samuel?'

Recognition: the insight step

In the examples, the teachers see what's going on. They pay attention not only to the children's games and how they do their work, but also to their social behaviour.

Often, a teacher only intervenes when the conflict is already under way. The first step is then to find out what the conflict is about by putting to both children questions that are as concrete as possible. If, for example, one of the children is crying, you ask both of them 'What's going on?' To the child who is crying you say: 'Do you have to cry like that, sweetie? What did he do? What do you want?' And you ask the other child: 'What did you want? Were you first on the chair? Did you want to play there? Come on, first we're going to comfort Anja and then we'll make a plan together.' Concrete questions are always much easier to understand than general questions such as: 'Why did you do that?' or 'How did that happen?' Future-directed questions (What do you want?) are also easier than historical questions about what happened.

Another probing strategy is a description and verification of the situation: 'You both want the train. Yes? Jessica, you've already taken Yasir's doll and now you are taking that cushion again? He made it so beautifully and you're going to throw it around?'

Later Branco gives the doll to the teacher

Adam comes up inquisitively and stands by the group

132

Resolution: the good idea step

The essence of the good-idea step is that the teacher hands children the suitable means to resolve their conflict. Good ideas come in all shapes and sizes. In one of our examples, the teacher asks Bridget how she feels ('Don't you like that?') and advises her to make her displeasure known to Anissa ('Then you should say so' says the teacher, and then to Bridget, 'Anissa doesn't like it.'). In the second example, the teacher explains what Samuel is actually doing ('He's only pointing. He wants to show what he has at home,'). She not only conveys to Megan the message that Samuel doesn't mean any harm, and that she can therefore let him do what he wants, but also suggests that he is trying to make contact with her. Her advice to Samuel is to the effect that there is a better way of making contact with Megan ('Say it then. You must ask, heh Samuel?').

Reconciliation: the step of restoring relations

Tools for gaining insight and finding solutions are necessary if the children are to find a way out of the conflict. They are keys that will open the door to restored harmony, but just as in *Alice in Wonderland*, children then find themselves in a room with new doors. These too have to be opened before they can be friends again. The teacher can help them to find the right keys for these doors. In the first place she must give them the feeling that the room beyond these doors is a place where you can have a really good time, that being friends again is the best thing there is. What this means is not just saying sorry, but acting sorry. Then you are friends again.

Branco gives Adam the doll

The teacher shows her pleasure at Branco's help

The three-step procedure is an important toolkit for the teacher herself, as soon as she steps into a conflict. But it is also important for the children that the teacher also has at her disposal the necessary tools to be able to key into their conflicts!

Every teacher's tool-kit should therefore contain the following three kinds of tools:

1. Tools that enable children to see where the other is coming from, and to get some insight into their own behaviour. The teacher can:
   - *ask after or point out the perspective of the two children:*
     (Thomas: 'Stupid David.') 'Now, I don't think David finds that very nice, do you? David, do you think that's nice? If she says stupid David, does that seem nice?' (David: 'No.') 'No, you see, it's not nice, is it?'
     'Look, Halil, the car drove right over her, that's why she's crying.'
     'If she doesn't want you to, then you mustn't do it, heh ?'
     'Joris wants to look for it himself.'
   - *consider what are the reasons for the behaviour (and sometimes verify them):*
     Alex has a conflict over a place on the seesaw. The teacher says Alex can sit between Noortje and Laura. She points to the left side and says: 'He could fall off there, because he can't hold on to anything.'
   - *identify and give names to emotions and behaviour and sometimes enforce the cardinal moral rule 'don't hurt each other':*
     'Surely you don't have to cry and fight at the same time?'
     'Because you're so angry, Lieve gets angry too.'
     'We don't pinch! What did we say, Laura, no, heh? It's not nice. You can ask, can't you?'

2. Tools that open for children the possibility of action toward resolving the problem. The teacher can:
   - *give an example of what precisely a child can do:*
     'Can he have another one? He wants the purple one. Give him that, then you can take the orange one back. Can he borrow the purple one? You'll get it back soon.'
   - *an alternative proposal:*
     'There are more chairs, Nouaman. Look, here's a chair. Come and get this one.'
     The teacher has told Cas he can set out the plates. Emma: 'No. I want the plates.' The teacher replies: 'Cas can do the plates, you do the knives.
   - *advice over saying or asking what they want:*
     'Then you say: Those are mine.'
     'You must ask: Can I get on? Go on, ask Wim.'

- *make a game of it*:
  When Shaya also wants a microphone, the teacher says: 'You can pretend you have one. Here, now you can sing.'
- *propose a compromise*:
  'Walid, Imane can have a go now, and then you.'
- *apply the rules*:
  Reciprocity: 'Jan let you have a go on the bicycle, now it's Jan's turn.'
  Equality: 'All children can have a slice of apple, not just you.'
  Individual right: 'Louise was given the motorcar for her birthday. It's hers.'
  Solidarity: 'Billy is still small: you have to help him if you're going to play together.'
  Giving and accepting direction: 'If you want to play, Niels, you must do what Fietje and Antje say.'

3. Tools that give children the possibility of making it up and being friends again. The teacher can:
   - *ask the children for a plan for how to become friends again or how to console a child.*
     'How can we cheer Rodni up again? Do you know a plan?'
   - *advise on how to do something that will make it up to a child:*
     'Give it to Rodni. He'll give it to Oussama.'
     'Go and help him stand up and then tell him you're sorry.'
   - *give advice on how to make it up through physical contact:*
     'Go and give her a kiss and say sorry?'
   - *give advice on going and doing something together:*
     'Look, Achmed can fit in here. There's room for Achmed too. There you are, you can lie here Achmed.'
     'Wim, Suzanne had the ball first. You can play together with Suzanne, too, can't you? If Suzanne puts the ball in first. Put the ball in first. Now Wim can have the ball, Give it to him. Now you play, go on.'
   - *compliment the children when they make it up:*
     'Well done,' says the teacher when Megan gives Samuel one of her crayons that they were earlier having a row over.
     'That's sweet of you. Say 'thank you ' when Branco gives up his duplo.'
   - *articulate in words what children do when they repair the relationship:*
     'Ah, look, Keenan is stroking you.'
   - *appeal to the unity of the whole group:*
     'It's so much nicer when everyone joins in together.'

In short:

- If you want to intervene in a conflict, think of the three-step procedure: *recognition, resolution* and *reconciliation*.
- Remember that the three-step procedure is not only important for yourself, but also for the children!
- Think of a way of introducing the three steps as a ritual.

29 Working magic with feelings

In the mediation process, the teacher tries to ensure that children are brought back into a positive relationship with each other. She is the good fairy in fairy tales. A good fairy knows that there is sometimes anger between children and that she cannot wholly prevent it. She is not omnipotent, but she can wave her magic wand. If a child is very angry and upset, she can give consolation. She can quieten savage children. And she can make all children and parents happy by giving them the feeling that they are welcome. How does she do it, this working magic with feelings?

Emotion theory

To help understand how people influence their own and others' feelings, we shall give a brief account of what scientists think about it (Frijda, 1986; Fischer, Shaver & Carnochan, 1990). The kernel of what they have to say is that emotion is energy, energy that is aroused by experience (stimuli) that affect us. This energy incites us to action. With positive stimuli we feel happy and our emotional actions are aimed at a closer approach (affectionately touching, looking inquisitively, holding fast), whereas negative stimuli evoke rejection (defence, attack, seeking help, crying, running away).

Young children react automatically when they are emotionally affected. Older children and adults can be aware of what they feel and why they feel it, and are able to choose between different ways of expressing the energy of their emotions. By expressing or not expressing their emotions, children can more and more deliberately influence their surroundings.

Managing children's emotions

When young children are powerfully affected by something, their emotional reactions are automatic. They need adults to help maintain an emotional balance, for without parents and teachers, they are at the mercy of their emotions. In groups where there are very many toys and little structure, for example, you sometimes see toddlers who appear almost drunk with all the impressions and simply don't know what they should do. These children are always stimulated by something else, to which they react automatically. This makes them undirected, unable to concentrate. Young children need teachers who can ensure that there is structure and there are limits, so that they can settle and concentrate somewhere.

The teacher can influence emotions by changing the surrounding stimuli. New play materials or a walk in the woods will always arouse curiosity. Reading aloud to a few children in the sleeping area is a good way to calm over-excited children.

Looking really sad and saying 'Oh, Janneke, a sore knee!' evokes the sympathy of the other children. The teacher can also provide and teach alternative ways of expressing emotions. 'If you're angry, don't hit, but say that you don't think it's fair.' And when children are really wild, the teacher knows that it will end in tears if she does nothing to release their energy. She can get them to sing together, for example, or get them marching round the room with arms outspread, being aeroplanes. The children can then get rid of excess energy, while the structured character of the exercise gives them something to hold on to, something that will restore calm. Comforting, cuddling and reading to young children are all ways of calming them, but the opposite approach works too: let them run around outside until they tire themselves out. Merely telling children 'Be quiet now' or 'Don't do that' is pointless. Young children need concrete guidance on how to act. Quiet, for example, is listening together on a mattress while the teacher reads a story to them, or drawing at a table.

Teaching children to direct their emotions themselves

There are some tricks that children themselves discover to influence their emotions. For example, finding comfort by sucking their thumb, or though a teddy bear or an old cloth. There is also an innate tendency to avoid unpleasant stimuli (because they give you feel a disagreeable feeling) and to seek out things that give a nice feeling. Young children know intuitively that distractions make you forget unpleasant feelings. A five year-old girl whose granddad had died refused to set foot in the room when everyone was crying and began to make strange jokes that she herself then laughed at with a hard, shrill laugh. Children from the age of four can already deliberately look for distraction when they feel wretched. But their fund of techniques for self-direction is still limited, and for this reason teachers and parents can teach children a great deal about working magic on their feelings.

Reconciliation: just touching

Branco knocks the tower down

The teacher makes a game of it too

- *Articulating feelings in words*

  Because young children very often act automatically, they cannot identify their feelings. They react angrily before they are aware of having angry feelings. It is the teacher teaching children to identify their feelings that enables them to escape from subjection to automatic action. By talking over what a child feels and what has made her upset, angry or confused, solutions can be sought. A pause for thought has been created between the stimulus and the automatic emotional reaction. If the teacher asks children what has made them upset or angry, and what they want, even with very young children, they can together look for a solution. The pause for thought created by talking also gives space to stop and consider the feelings of other children. What is it like to get a hard blow? What does a child feel if his fire-engine is snatched away from him? Putting into words what a child feels also quietens the child. This can even work with a baby that is upset because its mother has gone. With a soothing tone, a calm and melodious voice, the baby can be restored to well-being.

- *Be on the alert for the children's questioning look.*

  A young impulsive child cannot stop his or her behaviour alone. Such a child's behaviour is determined by stimuli from the surroundings, but at the same time the child often feels when things are not quite right. When children are uncertain, they look round with that special questioning look. If the teacher is alert and responds, the child learns to use the teacher as a moral guide.

- *Learning to talk to yourself*

  The teacher's 'No' reminds the child what is not allowed or what is dangerous. By saying what a child can do, attention and emotional energy are re-directed elsewhere. A year or more further on and the child can say 'No' to itself. This is known as the self-regulation of the emotions and self-control of behaviour.

  A striking example of this is the way in which the teacher Norien finally taught Cor (3;9) not to hit. In the playgroup Cor always reacted to anything he didn't like by hitting. Forbidding did nothing to help and the teachers were increasingly desperate and negative over Cor until Norien had an inspiration:

Reading aloud and talking about
animals and people

What dos the little girl want?

Norien (in a friendly but serious tone of voice): 'Come here. Which hand did you hit with?'

Cor: 'This one' (indicating his right hand).

Norien: 'Do you think it's a nice hand? Look at the hand.'

Cor: 'That's my hand.'

Norien: 'Do you like it? That hand hits and hurts children. Do you like that? Being hurt?'

Cor: 'No.'

Norien: 'What is that hand then?'

Cor: 'Naughty.'

Norien: 'Naughty hand, must not hit.'

Cor: 'Hand won't be naughty any more.'

Norien: 'No, of course not. Then you must keep a good watch on your hand.'

Cor skipped happily away full of good resolutions. Ten minutes later he returned to Norien.

Cor: 'Hand has been naughty again.'

And so there arose a bond of solidarity between Norien and Cor, to educate the hand together. And it worked. Cor learned to talk to himself and to control his hand.

- *Learning good manners*
  Every culture and every family has ways of dealing with strong emotions. When all is well, good manners help to express feelings. They offer protection against the threat of overwhelming emotions. Forcing children into the mould of predetermined, 'nice' behaviour no longer has a place in our present-day, but parents and teachers can certainly teach children good manners commensurate with their age and abilities. The custom of shaking hands can help children overcome shyness. Having a special chair to be quiet in can help children to get over their anger. Together with children you can think up manners for living with an ill child in the group. You can teach them manners to console another and manners to repair relations after a good clash. Creative activities can help children to give shape to their world of feeling – and, of course, talking instead of hitting and kicking!

- *Rituals of reconciliation*
  Teachers can also teach children rituals for reconciliation. Sometimes these are not rituals they have invented themselves but have taken them over from others, or they still remember them from their own childhood. Parents can also be a rich source of rituals; for example, never going to sleep after a row without first making it up. Such rituals can be verses, songs, shaking hands or always saying a friendly 'goodbye' when your parents come to fetch you. Rituals are culture-bound: in the Netherlands it is very normal to teach children to say 'sorry' or to give a kiss. In Russia (Bu-

tovskaya, Verbeek, Ljungberg en Lunardini, 2000) it was found that Russian children recited verses such as:

'Make it up, make it up,
don't fight, don't fight,
if you fight, then I'll bite,
and we mustn't bite because we're friends'.

They recited this together whilst holding each other's hands. Sometimes other children would come up and chant the verse to get them to stop quarrelling. It is the nature of rituals that they give an external form to feelings and insights without the meaning of the words and actions having to be clearly explicit. In the adult world too, for example in church or at a funeral, there are patterns in what is enacted that take their meaning from the fact that everyone knows them and knows when they are used. This is in fact the most important thing: knowing the use-value of rituals. Through their predictability they bring a kind of peace to specific occasions. Ritual is a means of staying on top of strong emotions, and rituals can have precisely the same function in the child day-care centre. Children grasp what rules and rituals stand for when they are clearly connected with the context in which they are used. They are like a spell through which the teacher can work magic with feelings. Dutch teachers also sometimes make up ritual verses or songs. Children love them.

I'm your friend, aren't I?

The children are sitting at a table. Cas (3;7) says to Leanne (3;2): 'I'm your friend, aren't I?' Leanne says 'yes', embraces Cas and gives him a kiss. The teacher says: 'Leanne, just a cuddle. Then let's sing the song about two friends?' At once all the children in pairs throw their arms round each other and the whole group sing the song about two friends.

- Arrange the surroundings or the time schedule such that particular emotions are evoked or given room for expression: a special place (corridor, hall or outside) for wildness; a corner with a sofa for rest; routines at fixed times, such as a music moment for gaiety, but also a surprise moment for curiosity and to avert boredom.

- Ensure a basic positive relationship, so that the child can always turn to you as a moral guide (e.g. the questioning look).

- Talk with the child about emotions, so that he or she learns to recognize his or her feelings.

- Give short, easily remembered rules, preferably in a language the child can use to talk to him/herself and to practise self-control ('Hand must not be naughty.').

- Talk with parents and colleagues about what 'good manners' the children should learn and how, together with the children, to give form to strong emotions.

30 Talking together

'Use words, use words!' called one of the teachers we observed when children resorted to physical violence in a quarrel. We encountered similar advice in many different variations: 'Then you say, "those are mine"'; 'or 'you should say, "I don't like that, Bill"'; or 'you must ask, "Can I have a go?"', and so on. But this injunction to 'use words!' is easier said by the teacher than put into practice by the children, especially young children who are only at the start of their language acquisition and do not yet possess many verbal tools. They do have words and they use sentences, but their meaning is not always what the teacher thinks it is. In learning to talk, children (and their educators) take three major steps: from play-talk to doing-talk to thinking-talk.

1. *Play-talking*

   In the first year, parents and teachers talk a great deal with babies, but for the babies this is at first no more than a pleasurable sound-game full of affection that is merely part of a sensory whole with all the touching and all the ways of being looked at. It's a form of contact, and the content hardly matters. In chapter 2 we showed how important this is for togetherness. When they are about nine months old, babies discover that the sounds of the play-talk can actually refer to something, that there is an intention behind it, that the sounds are relevant to the situation, that they *mean* something. This is the starting signal for the acquisition of the first words. Children make the first major step when they realize that words mean something.

You must say: I don't like that, Bill

He wants to show you what he has at home

2. Doing-talking

Children have to think themselves what words stand for and how word meanings are put together exactly but they already use them – in their own way – before they have fully worked this out. 'Their own way' includes their own form, their own meanings and sometimes formulae.

The first words are interwoven with the situation in which the child uses them.

That's mine

Cas, a one year-old, calls out, 'Tha's mine!' when he wants to take something away from Ricky, who is nearly two years old. Apparently another child said this to him in a thing-clash and for Cas this is now the formula for something like I-want-it-so-give-it. He at once understands the use-value. It's like a magical formula whose meaning-structure he will only later grasp.

Cas uses these words only in the context of getting hold of something. Children take their second major step when they grasp the word meaning freed from the particular situation. They then learn to use words in other situations and in other ways. Their language is then not merely about guiding and controlling what they do, or to express feelings of being ill at ease or happiness, or to get something done. It is increasingly about things that are not present in the here-and-now: over things that have either happened or should happen, over what is possible. But the things their words are about are still concrete things. They are still directly connected to their immediate environment.

When teachers intervene in conflicts, they should stay close to this concrete experience of doing. In the same way as working magic with feelings, as described in the last chapter, you should not say 'Be quiet', but rather 'Go quietly together and read a book on the mattress.' Play-talk becomes doing-talk, talk charged with an assignment to do something specific: 'Then you say: Those are mine', 'You must say: I don't like that, Bill.' A child can get to grips with this. To say that children must talk is only half the message: you must always also say what they can then do.

3. Think-talking

With the hoard of words they obtain in their second and third year, children can be very misleading. The words of young children are like rough diamonds that still have to be polished in the context of various sentences and situations before they have the richness of meaning of adult language. Think of Otto from chapter 17, our 'Champion of coercive seduction' who says 'together' when what he really means is: 'now me'. If the teacher allows herself to be deceived, then referring the conflict to the children's experience can make matters rather complicated, as in the following example:

Nico (3;7) screams.

Teacher: 'Abel, like that you, like that you are hurting Nico.'

Nico: 'He knocked the tent down. I don't want that and Thijs don't want that too.'

Teacher: 'Abel, perhaps you can, Abel can you please put the tent up again? Because you did that. Now, I'll help you Nico. I'll, I'll go and have a talk with Abel. Abel is not in the right frame of mind to listen. Abel, come over here. No, no, Abel. Abel, I want, Abel, calm down. You know what? I think that if you could play a bit more quietly, then Nico would really like to have you in the tent. Because he doesn't like it if you, if you keep on destroying the tent, then he wants you to go away. He doesn't want you, if you're rowdy, then Nico doesn't like that either. That's also why he doesn't want you in the tent. And if you play so wildly, then now and again you accidentally hurt someone. And Rian is Nico's friend. He doesn't like you hurting Rian and that's why he doesn't want to play with you. So just calm down, then it's easier for other children to play with you, OK? So let's have a quieter Abel.'

Abel (3;11): 'Then I'll go, I'll go, you know , then I'll go and play a game somewhere else.'

Teacher: 'That's a good idea.'

In this example, the teacher covers an enormous amount. She talks with Abel about:

- imagined-situations ('if you could play a bit more quietly, then Nico would really like to have you in the tent'; and 'if you play so wildly, you hurt Rian').
- Nico's feelings in this situation ('Nico would really like to have you in the tent.').
- the background to these feelings ('Rian is Nico's friend. He doesn't like you hurting Rian and that's why he doesn't want to play with you.').
- Nico's wishes ('if you keep on destroying the tent, then he wants you to go away.').

Her lecture is based on the assumption that Abel is capable of reconstructing the whole story through her language, with its sequence of logical connections (if..., then...) and that he can connect various word meanings with each other (quiet – rowdy; doesn't like – hurting). What she demands from Abel is that he should think through the scenario she presents with her words. What she is doing is using think-talk: talk that carries an assignment not to go and do something but to think about something. This is the third major step in language development. Children take the third step when they learn to reflect with their language, when with their language they can imagine scenarios that make them more aware of what they are doing and what they could do. Words then really do become tools to control behaviour and emotions, and then very gradually children also learn how to practise magic with words. In the stage of think-talking, language becomes increasingly an instrument for reflecting on practical action and on the thoughts and feelings related to it. The laboured account that Abel's teacher presents to him is difficult because it is so long. When teachers talk a lot with children they know intuitively what the zone of proximal development is at the time. It is very important that the teacher should always be one step in front of the children in her language use. Children pick up from it what they can use and when they are working on this they give developmental signals that the teacher can read. A teacher who looks and listens well and makes the connection with her language is passing on to them her magic wand.

Pedagogical tips to remember

Teachers can help children take the steps from play-talk to doing-talk to thinking-talk.

- At each step: when you talk, keep you eyes and ears open.
- Make sure that your words do not stray too far from what the children are actually doing.
- Bear in mind that children can interpret words differently than a teacher intends.
- Children can discover all kinds of things from your language: give them the chance to develop their thinking-talk.

Part 6

DIVERSITY

31 Differences between children

Every teacher knows that no child is alike. For some children, everything goes swimmingly. True, they have their clashes, but these are over before the teacher has to get involved. Other children constantly demand attention because there is almost always something going on with them. Sometimes it's small groups of children getting in the way of others. The art of the teacher is on the one hand to take account of individual differences and to give each child personal attention, and on the other hand to be alert to relations between children and the group as a whole. Moreover, the teacher has the pedagogical task of teaching young children to deal with differences between children. This presents teachers with two related questions:

1. How can I help children play together when they are very different in certain respects? For instance, how can I let children play together when they are at very different stages of development? How can I help them if they have so many conflicts that they absorb all my attention and disrupt the whole group? How can I organise play together with boys who demand a great deal of room and don't much care for the less robust games - like doing puzzles - which call for finer motor skills? How can I get children, who at home have different customs, values and norms, to join in playing together?

2. How can I make sure that I keep an open mind and am not misled by prejudices? For example, How to keep an open mind rather than assuming that the older child is always to blame in a conflict because he should have known better; an open mind instead of thinking every time there is conflict, 'is that wretched boy causing another row' without investigating to see who is responsible this time. Everyone has images of boys and girls, of 'people like me' and (children of) parents with different ethnic backgrounds. It's always a question of differences that you assume between children and the way you interpret differences. We'll try to make this clear with an example:

Jaoud (3;7) of Moroccan origin and Pablo (2;3) whose parents are Spanish, often get in each other's way. At a certain moment the teacher sees that Pablo has reacted to this very impulsively by trying to seize the motorcar that Jaoud is playing with. Jaoud reacts by warding him off and protests, but does not allow the situation to escalate into a row.

What is actually going on here? Is this a conflict between a young, impulsive child and an older, wiser child who knows that his younger friend doesn't yet fully understand how to behave? Or is Pablo a difficult little boy, possibly even an ADHD-child? On a first analysis of part of our material, it seemed that the conflicts of Moroccan children were more often minor incidents ('mishaps') than those of children from other ethnic groups. Is this related to ethnic difference, we asked ourselves? But subsequent analysis of all the data showed that there were no significant differences. How would we have interpreted the children's behaviour if Jaoud had been a girl?

The individual approach

Many teachers will respond to these questions by saying that it makes no difference whether Jaoud is a boy or a girl, a Dutch or a Moroccan child. It's a question of the individual child, they say, not representatives of this or that group. Because every child has his or her own idiosyncrasies, which are not really affected by sex, culture or age, they are unwilling to differentiate. Their experience with children who are always having conflicts has taught them that first and foremost they should look at the background of the individual child: why is it that this particular child is so difficult? What kind of temperament does the child have? Is there perhaps something wrong with the situation at home? Is there something wrong with the child itself?

Starting points for this approach:

Think of all children as individuals.
- Only pay attention to personal character features: shyness, being wild or sociable, and so on. Act on the basis of children's personality characteristics.
- Work at good practice for everyone.

Diversity in pedagogical approach

There are also teachers who especially concern themselves with the relationships between the children. According to them, the approach to the individual falls short, because what children above all need to learn is to get along with real differences and the inequalities related to them. Older children are more capable and can be allowed to be dominant if this works positively for the children. Inequality in a situation, even inequality in a relationship between children, need not necessarily be a bad thing. What these teachers are anxious about are disruptions of the togetherness of the group. They are worried about disruptions that (can) have to do with differences in age, sex, social skills or language mastery. What they watch out for is the impotence of children that leads to negative patterns of behaviour. They are aware that situations like that of Jaoud and Pablo are like objects viewed through a kaleidoscope – they know that there are always multiple perspectives from which events in the group can be viewed, each one showing a different pattern. For this reason they do not judge from a single perspective - 'he is so young', 'she is such a smart-ass', 'that's the ADHD for you' and so on.

Is it a case of conflict where one child is impotent in the face of the claims of the older? Or is it about the forcefulness of the big boy? Or is it that the child of Dutch origin has the upper hand because he speaks better Dutch? Or is it perhaps that one child is Dutch, older and stronger all at once? Is one child constantly worsted by an older child, of the other sex etc.?

In the day-care centre too, children develop their own culture. They might create a negative culture in which, for instance, an issue arises of certain girls against boys, a group of older against younger children, a few socially adept children against a clumsy child, or a few linguistically advanced against linguistically backward children. In a diversity approach, the teacher tries to prevent these kinds of group attitudes arising. She can decide whether she wants to take these group differences as an opportunity to teach children to be socially responsible: getting an older child to help a younger child, or finding a language-mate for a new child who doesn't yet speak the language of the day-care centre. The teacher knows that what the children bring with them from home also plays a part. Talking with parents is a way to grasp other perspectives with which she can then vary the way she sees relations between children in the kaleidoscope.

Starting points for this approach:

- Develop feelers, antennae, and keep an alarm bell that will ring when you think you detect negative patterns that have to do with age, sex, ethnicity or a child's social-emotional problems.
- Think of children as actively working on their relations with others and give attention to the needs of all parties if negative patterns do arise between groups of children.
- Think of yourself as the director of a play about helping each other and showing what you can do, a director who, out of the social differences of your actors, creates the possibility of playing glorious roles.

The chapters in this section have been written from the viewpoint of this diversity approach.

This approach is attentive to the relations between the children and to the assumption of (negative) images. Our first advice, before all else, is: look, look, look! Look for the logic in children's actions. Look for the logic in their actions as this develops in the group or between groups. Look out for your own preconceived ideas that can get in the way of looking properly at the idiosyncrasies of individual children. Look too at what parents see.

32 Younger and older children

Children learn from each other. This is a good reason for placing younger children together with older children in the same group. Children can then participate in the whole cycle: from being the youngest, who still has everything to learn, to being the eldest in the group. The youngest can learn to accept guidance and direction from the eldest. The clashes that arise from time to time between older and younger children reveal those points at which they sometimes irritate or fail to understand each other and where assistance is needed.

Older children don't want the attention of the younger children

Kristel (2;7) is sitting next to Shaznay (3;10) chalking on the square. Kristel puts a stripe across one of Shaznay's tiles and looks at her, laughing. Shaznay does not react and Kristel chalks another stripe across her tile, throwing a questioning look at Shaznay, who now responds, pushing Kristel's arm away and looking at her crossly: 'What are you doing? That's mine!' Kristel is taken aback by Shaznay's fierce reaction and looks at her perplexedly. Let's try one more time: Kristel carefully chalks a stripe and looks anxiously in Shaznay's direction. Shaznay returns the look but further ignores Kristel by turning away and going on with her drawing. Kristel finally seems to get the message that Shaznay is not interested in communal drawing. Kristel stands up and walks off.

Wim snatches the house

The teacher explains: you can play together as well

Wim and the power of the little one

Cecile (3;4) and Suzanne (3;2) are playing with a house that you can roll a ball through. Wim (2;4) comes across to Suzanne and tries to grab the ball from her. Suzanne resists and looks to the teacher. Wim tries with all his might to prise her fingers apart and then he too casts a questioning look toward the teacher and camera. A wrestling match then ensues with blows, pushing and pulling and possibly an attempt at biting by Wim. Now the teacher spots what's going on: 'Wim, no biting! Who had the ball first?' 'I had it first,' says Suzanne. The teacher pulls Wim away from Suzanne and says: 'You can play together with Suzanne, can't you? If Suzanne puts the ball in first.' The teacher then explains the game, while Suzanne throws the ball through the hole. As soon as the ball emerges from the house, Wim pounces on it. 'Not so fast! Just wait!' says the teacher and pulls Wim away. Suzanne is allowed another go at rolling the ball through the house and then Wim can have his go. The teacher explains once more how to play the game. It works, and Wim crows with pleasure. The teacher has to leave to see to other children's needs. At first it goes well, taking turns, but then the conflict starts up again.Wim grabs the house and ball from Cecile and rolls the ball. Cecile: 'Can I?' Wim: 'Nooooo!' The teacher calls from a distance: 'Wim, what did we say?' Wim looks at the teacher and pushes the house over to Cecile. He indicates to Cecile where the ball has to go and then stands stamping and chafing until it's his turn again. But Cecile has other ideas: Suzanne should also be allowed another turn. She tries to get hold of the house for her friend, which leads to further wrestling and the girls tease Wim. The teacher has had to go and assist in the adjacent toilet area, and so cannot admonish them. Then Wim resorts to his ultimate weapon: he bites. The result is two crying children, a third looking rather appalled, and a camerawoman and teacher who rush over to give consolation.

Cecille gives the house to Suzanne

Wim wrestles over the house

Being much stronger is nice

Jasmijn (2;8) and Otje (2;1) are playing on the roof of a play-house. When Chèrie climbs up the stairs, they quickly go and sit in front of the entrance to block her way. When this works they laugh, but then Sam (3;11) arrives. First he pushes Chèrie aside, then both the younger children and then starts wrestling with Otje. Very quickly Otje finds himself on his back. When Sam begins to kick, Otje kicks back and Chèrie also joins in kicking with Sam. Then Sam says: 'Quick, downstairs!' Sam, Jasmijn and Chèrie scamper down the stairs, laughing, career round the room and then back again to Otje. Once more Otje is given a roughing-up and then again the threesome run round the room shrieking with pleasure. When they again charge at Otje, he is sitting on the stairs. Sam hits Otje with a large teddy bear but Chèrie hits him with a teatray and Otje suffers a hard crack over the fingers. This is too much for Otje and he at once starts to cry. Alarmed, the teacher hurries over and comforts Otje. Sam is cross with Chèrie because she has hurt Otje. With an unhappy, guilty face and with bowed head Chèrie walks away.

The stay-away-from-me feeling

Younger children are often very curious about older children's games. They try to attract the older children's attention, for example by touching the things they are playing with. When the older child is concentrating on his play, such attention is by no means welcome and can lead to a 'stay-away-from-me' clash. This kind of clash is as a rule very short-lived, with the younger child learning the rule: don't disturb.

Impulsive and difficult to control

Impulsive and enthusiastic children like Wim are more difficult. Wim's desire is so strong and he simply can't stop himself. Moreover, he has discovered biting. Biting and attracting the teacher's attention by crying are the weapons of the youngest children. What the example shows is that with the

Wim resorts to his ultimate weapon   Two crying children and a third, an appalled   Wim, and the teacher Ronald

teacher's assistance Wim can watch the game and control himself, and that he can maintain this even after the teacher's departure. These are the positive points to emphasise and to work on. What more could the teacher have done? Perhaps he could have given the two girls some guidance; he could have got the girls to explain and show how to play and he could have said to the girls and to Wim that they were in charge because they were older and already knew how to play. But even in that case, it probably needed the teacher to remain close at hand to back up the girls should Wim's desire and enthusiasm threaten to get the better of him again.

Impulsive children need help in:
- learning to look and learning to grasp what other children are doing. This can be done by watching together with them and talking about what the others are doing.
- learning to stop and to control themselves. This can be done by immediately correcting the child and reminding them of the rule, telling them as concretely as possible what they should do and praising them when they do it well. It helps to teach other, older children the rules as well.

Power is wonderful

One of the first things new children learn is that stronger children can boss younger children about. Naturally, neither teachers nor parents approve of this; but when we look at our research it simply is the reality. Children discover their power. It is one of the tasks of teachers to teach children positively to deal with differences in power. How you do this is a question over which parents and teachers can differ strongly in their opinions. The following views emerged from our interviews with mothers:
- You have to teach children to hit back.
- Children should call the teacher or mother when something is unfair.
- You have to ignore whining, otherwise children learn to manipulate the teacher.
- Children who enjoy power are abnormal.
- For their own safety, children should learn that the law of the strongest often holds good.
- The rule that stands above and before everything else is: 'Don't hurt each other.'
- Older children have to learn to help younger children and so to be responsible.

In our research, we witnessed examples of older children positively guiding younger children by making eye contact, fixing their attention on something, demonstrating how to do something and then inviting the young child to imitate them, to laugh or to put into words what he or she is doing. We cannot, however, say how frequently this occurs. Research into positive leadership among two- and three-year-olds is still in its infancy. We do think that encouraging positive leadership is a good way for children who enjoy power, or who are bossy with younger children, to learn how to exercise their power. We would suggest having a serious talk with Sam and Chèrie in which the teacher discussed with them their behaviour toward Otje – a conversation in which she explained that they are much bigger and stronger than Otje, that being bigger and stronger is a wonderful thing because you can do all kinds of things that smaller children still have to learn, but that it also brings with it responsibility. Bigger children have to help smaller or weaker children when they need it. The teacher should finally be able to ask Sam and Chèrie whether they have any idea of how they can help Otje.

Pedagogical tips to remember

- Protect older children against being disturbed too often by younger children.

- Confirm the need of older children to be big and strong and try to tie this to a sense of responsibility toward younger children.

33 Children with many conflicts

In every childcare centre there are children who are always clashing with other children and often enough with teachers too. What to do with them?

The scapegoat

According to the teachers, Niels (3;11) is an ADHD-child, easily distracted and easily irritated. Niels has been playing for some time with a tractor when Benno tries to take it away from him. Niels reacts angrily. They both hold onto the tractor and scream. This brings the teacher on the scene. 'What's going on?' she asks, taking hold of Niels' arm. 'You have to play together, heh? Benno can play as well.' She gives Benno some other toy and Niels continues playing with the tractor. But then the teacher says: 'Benno can drive the car too, not just you.' Benno doesn't wait to hear this twice but pitches in and grabs the tractor, screaming. A fight breaks out. The teacher responds to this by speaking angrily and dismissively to Niels: 'Don't fight!' Benno lets go of the tractor but as soon as the teacher is gone, he at once throws himself on the tractor again. The fight starts all over again, while in the background the teacher shouts: 'Niels!'

The correcting, consoling, binding teacher

Theo (3;2) is another child who has many conflicts in the day-care group. According to the teachers, there are lots of problems at home. A clash begins when Theo looks through a little window and Bert (3;4) and Tineke (2;11) also want to have a look. Theo spreads his arms and blocks their view, and subsequently he hits and kicks them. In tears, Tineke calls for the teacher. The teacher takes Theo by the hand in a friendly manner, leads him away from the window and says to him very clearly, but in a positive tone of voice: 'Listen, Theo. You mustn't do that. You must not kick other children. You must not hurt them.' She squats on her haunches behind the children as she says this. Theo submits and tries to go and stand between the two children. Then he starts crying: '...c-can't see.' He goes and sits on the teacher's lap, while she strokes him and tries to console him. Theo then says: 'I want Mummy.' The teacher corroborates his longing for his mother: 'Yes, soon you'll be able to see Mummy, but now I'm so glad to have you with me. Soon you'll go home to Mummy.' She turns Theo on her lap so that he faces the direction of the window, where Bert and Tineke remain looking and talking over what they see. The teacher begins to talk with them and involves Theo too, while at the same time continuing to stroke him. In this way she helps Theo to restore relations and to join in again with the others.

Reflex patterns

Theo was lucky to have a teacher who could show firmness with kid gloves. She consoles, changing the anger to sorrow, and as a result he is able to calm down. She then helps him to restore contact with the other children. We filmed Theo again six months later, by which time he was having far fewer clashes. According to the teachers, he still needed a lot of extra attention, but things were going much better in the group. The other children were no longer afraid of him and even wanted to play with him. Niels, on the other hand, had no such luck. After 'two years of Niels' the teachers were fed up with him because he never listened, he rowed constantly and screamed at the least provocation. They explained his behaviour as due ADHD, but they never looked at their own role in the problem. Teachers and parents often unconsciously mirror the behaviour of children and serve to reinforce it as a result:

• A quiet, reserved child is forgotten. People withdraw from the child.
• A child who hits, kicks and screams encounters a lot of screaming angry people.
• A child who is seriously restless and fidgety makes others restless and fidgety.
• A child who talks and converses happily meets people who enjoy talking to him.

It is part of the professionalism of the teacher to see through these reflex patterns and to break them. It is precisely with the difficult children that teachers are in danger of developing behavioural difficulties themselves. Singer (2002) found that in the conflicts of children who were frequently involved in conflicts, the teachers themselves almost always displayed inadequate behaviour, such as giving contradictory messages, finding a scapegoat, exhibiting a negative attitude toward one child, responding minimally or leaving children to their fate.

An additional problem for children with behavioural difficulties is that the other children are quick to seize on it if that child always gets the blame from the teacher. For instance, they know they can then take things away from that child or push him around without being punished. We have seen this on various occasions. But it is precisely with these children, who, for whatever reason, are difficult to get along with, that the teacher can make a great difference: either by amplifying the problems or by helping them positively to connect with other children.

Pedagogical tips to remember

When an aura of negativity develops around a child – too many clashes with other children and with the teacher – ask a colleague or assistant to make a video of what is going on and to observe closely:

- *Negative spirals*: behaviour from the teacher that unintentionally reinforces the child's negative behaviour, or behaviour by the child that is exploited by other children or that they find a nuisance.

- *Forming negative images*: if it is always assumed that a particular child is the guilty party whenever he is involved in a conflict (he is the scapegoat), this becomes a self-fulfilling prophecy. In the end, the child will behave as predicted: he will be the guilty one. It is therefore very important to correct negative images as soon as they begin to form.

- *Positive starting points*: situations where these problems don't arise. What kind of situations might these be? What can we learn from this for the situations where problems do arise?

Remember that you're not the only one who has failed to emerge successful from a disastrous power struggle with a child. If your attempts to pursue a positive approach don't work out, seek the support of colleagues and together, in consultation with the parents, try to think of how to try another tack.

34 Girls and boys

Boys and girls: are they the same or different? It's a question that will always guarantee a lively discussion. Some think that there are already clear differences at two or three years of age, others dispute it. We find this disagreement among developmental psychologists as well as teachers, and among Moroccan, as well as Dutch mothers. What have our observations shown about the children in our research?

Looking for something exciting

Samuel (boy, 3;2) is in a group of fourteen children. Today it's impossible to play outdoors. Together with other children, Samuel has been drawing with crayons on the board and is now walking around looking for something new. With an inflatable ball in his mouth, he walks toward the table where Jaydin (girl, 3;2) en Chavaro (boy, 3;8) are playing happy families together with the teacher. Samuel wants to take a card lying in front of Jaydin but Jaydin pushes him quickly though firmly away. Then Samuel takes a chair, shoves it in Jaydin's direction and says: 'Play cards?' Immediately he takes the card lying in front of Jaydin and then another one. 'Nooo!' an irritated Jaydin turns round and tries to take back the cards from Samuel's hand. Samuel resists and holds the cards behind his back. 'Give it!' shrieks Jaydin and thumps him on the shoulder. To the teacher she says: 'He's taken them from me!' The teacher mediates and Jaydin gets her cards back. Samuel walks away.

Samuel is on the prowl, Jaydin pushes him away

Samuel tries to snatch Jaydin's puzzle, Jaydin snatches it back

1 minute later

Samuel puts his puzzle on the table and goes to sit next to Chavaro and Jaydin. Chavaro shoves Samuel's puzzle away. 'Nooo!' shouts Samuel and pulls his puzzle back toward himself. Chavaro does not react, gives the teacher a look and remains sitting at the table.

1 minute later

While Jaydin is talking to the teacher, Samuel takes the box that the cards came from. Jaydin doesn't notice, but another teacher does and calls: 'Samuel, Samuel, what are you doing?' Surprised, Samuel looks questioningly toward the teacher and picks up the other half of the box. Now Jaydin sees clearly what he is doing. 'Give it to me! Those are mine.' Jaydin takes her things back and looks toward the teacher. Samuel walks away from the table and toward another group of children in another corner.

30 seconds later

Samuel walks up and takes the lady's bag from which Megan (girl, 2;9) has been inseparable the whole day. Megan is shocked, says 'No!' and tries to pull the bag out of Samuel's hands. But Samuel won't let go, he looks frustrated and the two children end up wrestling for possession. Megan has a telephone in her hand and hits Samuel's hand with it, but Samuel, grim-faced, holds on the bag. Megan then raises her arm and gives him a hefty blow to the head with the telephone. That hurts! Samuel holds his head and runs crying to the teacher. The teacher comforts Samuel and talks in a conciliatory manner with both children. Then she leads Samuel back to the table with puzzles and they do a puzzle together.

10 minutes later

Samuel is doing his puzzle. Then up walks Megan, lays her lady's bag on the table and tries to grab one of the pieces of Samuel's puzzle. Chavaro tries to restrain her arm but Megan persists. Samuel protests: 'No! That's mine.' Together with Chavaro he tries to pull the piece out of Megan's hand. Megan tries to get help from the teacher, but she says: 'No, Megan, just as he was not allowed to have your telephone.' Megan walks angrily away from the table. 'Yea, Yea!' shouts a jubilant Samuel and goes back to work on the puzzle with the teacher.

Samuel walks away...

and finishes up in another row

Happily, he can come and do a puzzle with the teacher

A few patterns

In our research we found boys and girls equally often involved in rows. Boys were no rougher than girls. All the children went in for pulling, pushing and hitting in order to get their own way, regardless of gender. Both sexes were capable of resolving conflicts through talking.

But we also found a few clear differences between boys and girls. Boys more frequently clashed when they were seeking a new activity, like Samuel in the case above. Girls more often had clashes when they were playing together, especially in the dolls and dressing-up corners. The girls talk more in order to resolve their conflicts. In addition, when they have a conflict with another girl, girls are found to be more oriented toward finding a solution than when they have a conflict with a boy, or when boys have conflicts between each other.

How can we explain these differences? The fact that boys have more clashes when they are looking for a new activity may arise from a greater need for movement. Playing inside with puzzles, card games, drawing with crayons etc. can make them restless, and as a result they tend to wander about and disturb other children. This would explain Samuel's behaviour. A number of researchers have shown that boys want to run more, race, wrestle, scream and cycle more: robust games involving lots of movement through which they can work off their energy. Another difference that has often been noted is that girls play more with dolls, toy tea sets and dressing up. It is only logical that that they clash more with girls there than with boys. It does not often occur that boys clash with each other in the dolls' corner. Playing close together in the dolls' corner could also explain the tendency of girls to find solutions together. If you are forced to play close by each other in the confined space of a dolls' house, you often have to find your way out of problems, and this you do frequently by negotiation.

Suppose these explanations are correct, what would it mean for the pedagogical approach of teachers? According to the Australian researcher Glenda McNaughton (2000), teachers should protect girls against wild, obtrusive, pushy boys who disturb their play with puzzles, dolls and scissors and paste. Otherwise boys learn that dominant macho behaviour is okay. The Dutch researchers Lauk Woltering and Louis Tavecchio (2005) stick up for the boys: they need more room and preferably men as teachers with whom they can wrestle and play jokes.

Thinking about boys and girls getting along together, it seems to us that the following points are worth noting. Research shows that although boys and girls at the age of two to three years already have different play preferences, both sexes also resemble each other a great deal. There are also girls who love running and racing around and boys who prefer less robust, quieter or more skilful games. From two years of age, however, children begin to develop a preference for playing with members of their own sex, although playing separately does not as a rule become clearly evident until four of five years of age. This probably happens because children would rather play with other children who like the same things as they do and are good at them. It would seem best for child day-care to try to give children sufficient room – both literally, so that they can run freely where they don't disturb others, and figuratively, so that they can follow their own preferences. If we can do this, we will be giving them the room for their talents to unfold and for them to widen their repertoire.

Finally, it is most important to be aware that everyone is seeing children through gender-tinted spectacles. Without being conscious of it, we have ideas about what is normal for girls and for boys, and we treat them accordingly. We reward, punish, correct and encourage on the basis of these gender stereotypes, often wholly unaware of it. We need to pay more attention to this.

Pedagogical tips to remember

- Ensure that both quieter and more energetic children can find what they want by providing a range of play materials and the use of both indoor and outdoor space.

- Avoid the trap of thinking in negative gender stereotypes when children have many clashes, but rather look to see what the needs of each individual child are.

- A bell should start ringing whenever you begin thinking in such terms as: prissy girl behaviour, a catty female, boys monkeying about, and macho behaviour etc. But be fair too: We have yet to meet the first person who has never had unpleasant thoughts over the opposite or even their own sex.

35 Children from different cultural and ethnic backgrounds

At many child centres, children from different cultural and ethnic backgrounds play together. Does this difference affect the children? How do teachers deal with the differences?

What do young children do?

Most two- and three-year-old children are not aware that the culture of other children at home can be different from their own. Nor are they aware that they belong to different groups of the population because their (grand)parents were born in a different country from their own (grand)parents. Certainly, they can see external differences but they have as yet formed no stereotyped image on the basis of such difference, as older children and adults often have done. The age at which children learn to notice and evaluate these differences is between three and five years, when they learn to evaluate differences in a positive or negative sense. It may then be a matter of differences between rich and poor, boy and girl or difference in ethnicity and ethnic origin (Raundalen, Mac Naughton & Vandenbroeck, 2004).

But how is this manifest in their behaviour: do young children already have different habits related to the way they behave with each other at home? Do children from different ethnic backgrounds behave differently in conflict situations? As far as we looked at these questions in our research, the answer is very clear: in general, not at all. The West Indian, Moroccan and Dutch children in our investigations have roughly the same frequency of conflicts, which are in the same proportions mishaps, disagreements or rows. There are no differences relating to the type of the conflict: they clash equally often over objects or over wanting to join in. There are also many similarities in the way they then behave. If we look at the averages for the whole group, whether children direct others, sense what the other is going to do, or resolve conflicts, there is no difference.

But that is not to say that all behaviour is the same. The conflicts of Dutch children last longest (24 seconds) and those of Moroccan children are the soonest over (16 seconds); an average difference of 8 seconds. It is difficult to say how this comes about. Are Dutch children sometimes more stubborn when they want something, or are they more robust in negotiation ? Do the Moroccan children give up sooner? There is one difference that could perhaps contribute to the length of conflicts: the Dutch children seem to take more time to answer and explain, to respond nicely or to laugh and also to make it up together again. Perhaps they are brought up in more of a talking culture than the Moroccan children. (Pels 1991).

What do teachers do?

Although the teachers intervene with roughly the same frequency in the conflicts of children from different ethnic backgrounds, we did notice differences in the way in which they did this. The teachers used more power strategies when mediating in conflicts of the Moroccan children than in those of the Dutch or West Indians. The following examples illustrate this difference:

Leave it alone

Walid (2;8) and Aiemane (3;3), both of Moroccan origin, are playing with blocks in the vicinity of a motorcar. Walid stands up and seizes the car. 'Ahhh!' shouts Aiemane and he too takes hold of the car, pushing Walid away. The teacher, who sits a little further away, calls: 'Aiemane, Aiemane, leave it alone!' Aiemane and Walid both let go of the motorcar. 'Now Walid can have it', says the teacher.

Did he take it?

A group of children are playing with duplo. Gianni (2;2), Dutch-Hindustani, takes duplo from the Dutch boy Branco (2;7), in the process of clearing up. Branco protests: 'Eeeeh!' The teacher has just arrived on the scene and says: 'Did he take it? Then say: "It's mine." Branco says, "Mine", quietly.' The teacher looks at Gianni and says: 'I think Branco made it.' Gianni walks toward Branco who holds out his hands, but then he turns round again. Branco again protests: 'Ehhh!' 'Hey, you little rogue, a piece?' and the teacher pokes Gianni in the belly with her finger and laughs. 'Or else make it new, Branco,' she says. 'Look, go and make a new one. This is bigger,' and she picks up a duplo-tower and puts it down for Branco. 'This is nicer.'

This difference in approach is not due to differences in behaviour between the children, since we found no differences in directive or mediating behaviour on the part of the children themselves. How do we explain it? In chapter 33, about children who often clash with other children, we saw that the teacher sometimes mirrors the children's behaviour and reinforces it as a result. She observes the child's behaviour and reacts to it. But sometimes the teacher is reacting not so much to the specific behaviour of the child in question at that moment, but on the basis of an image or a stereotypic idea, in which case it's prejudice at work. Perhaps it's that the image the teacher has of Moroccan children in conflict situations is misrepresented through differences in their use of language. When the Moroccan children mediate, their sentences are shorter than those of Dutch children, although the import of the sentences can be exactly the same:

Here, take this

Soukaina (3;4), a Moroccan girl, is playing with a puzzle. Chiney (3;4) does something with Soukaina's puzzle and Soukaina shouts: 'Hey!' Chiney repeats her action: 'So, so.' Soukaina pushes her arm away and then says: 'Here, take this,' and pushes another puzzle over to her.

I'll go and find one for you

Timo (3;6), a Dutch boy, is playing with Jordy in the building corner. Timo takes a block that lay on the ground in front of Jordy: 'Hey, I need that one.' 'No!' shouts Jordy. Timo points to the cupboard where the blocks are kept. 'There's another one,' he says. 'No, no, that one was mine!' responds Jordy, to which Timo replies: 'I'll go and find one for you,' and walks over to the cupboard with the blocks to get one for Jordy.

The different language use of the Moroccan children could be the reason the teacher addresses them at a rather lower developmental level. In an investigation of Scottish infant schools, the researchers looked to see whether the same teachers systematically discriminated between Scottish children and children of the same age and sex but of Indian and Pakistani origin (Ogilvy, Boath, Cheyne, Jahoda and Schaffer, 1992). The level of mastery of the English language was lower for the Asian children than for the Scots. It was found that their teachers systematically approached the children differently, and systematically to the disadvantage of the Asian children. The teachers had a style that was rather similar to that which we found with our teachers of the Moroccan children: they were more directive, responded negatively more frequently and treated their request for attention more superficially. They put more open questions to the Scottish children and dealt with their questions more thoroughly, whereas their conversations with the Asian children revealed their assumption that this would be too difficult for them. This meant that the Asian children got fewer chances to develop their language through interaction with their teachers. Adapting to their level, or adapting to an *idea* of their level, thus had exactly the wrong effect. If the same is true for Moroccan children, it means that their teachers are short-changing them. The lesson to be drawn from these results is that the teacher should connect with less linguistically skilled children at their potential rather than their actual level!

Pedagogical tips to remember

- Regard all children as individuals, no matter how young they are: Two- and three-year-olds are already whole personalities! Even when averages are found that show statistical differences between ethnic groups, no individual person is an average.

- Beware of negative spirals. Mirroring the behaviour of children can lead to exactly the undesired result. The level of (Dutch) language mastery is sometimes misleading as to what children can do. Try therefore to get an insight into their intentions. Talk with all children in an enriching way: put questions to them, give them room and let them talk, follow up what children say.

- Beware of stereotypic ideas and of estimating children too low. It can damage children's ability to develop. Try to connect with what children can do and what seems within their reach. Start from what they can learn.

36 Similarities and differences between parents

All parents want their children to become respectful adults who are considerate of others and can abide by rules. Many parents share the same objectives in the upbringing of their children, but there is less agreement on how to achieve these aims. Indeed, there are major differences of pedagogical approach, and so when it comes to conflicts between children parents react very differently.

We let mothers themselves – after showing them a video-clip – tell how they would have reacted in the filmed conflict situation which escalated to hitting and kicking and ended with a little boy crying loudly. The teacher had seen nothing and arrived as soon as she heard the boy crying.

A Dutch mother:

> 'Why does the teacher do nothing? I certainly wouldn't have allowed kicking and hitting '
>
> 'What I would do: I would separate them. I'd put them in different chairs and let them to play together only after a quarter of an hour or more. Then I would explain to the children why that's not allowed and ask them: 'Why did you do that?' What I'd want to achieve is that they would go and reflect on what they'd done. I think giving explanations is very important, because otherwise children think that what they did was OK; and because otherwise they don't understand why they've been punished; and because then they're going to sit there and think: 'Why am I sitting here?''

A Moroccan mother:

> 'I don't agree at all that the teacher should only look after the little boy who's crying. When you only comfort the victim you create feelings of hostility within the group of children. They see that she comforts the child, gives him attention, cuddles him and picks him up, and that creates jealousy among the children. Then they don't understand what's going on. She should talk with them too and discuss the problem with them. I think she should give attention to all the children and involve them all, not just the victim, but also the culprits, so that they know that they're also valued as persons. Otherwise they won't understand that.'

A West Indian mother:

> 'Yes, I can see Ivaron [her son] in that child. It's not good to teach a child to hit others, but Ivaron is a child like the little boy who was hit, and that's why I've told him that if another child hits him he should hit him back. Why did I do that? Ivaron has to be able to defend himself so that they don't walk all over him.'
>
> 'What I would do is first get the attention of the other children. I would put the children who were kicking on one side and say that they must not do what they did. They must play together and be nice to each other. They must be good to each other. Playing together is really important. That's how they learn to get on with people. They learn to get on with other children and to play.'

The Dutch mother in this example would prefer to intervene in the conflict earlier than did the teacher on the video. She would separate the children and explain why she does not like this behaviour. After that, she would talk with the children and ask them to explain what happened. She combines directive and mediating approaches with the aim that the children shall learn that this is not permitted and that there are rules and norms that they have to conform to. For her, the conflict is a moral problem.

The Moroccan mother in this example looks at the whole group of children. In her view, all the children – both victims and perpetrators – should get attention and that in the end they should all have to play together again. She looks at the emotions of all the children concerned. Hers is a mediating approach and what she wants to achieve by it is that every child should feel seen and valued.

The West Indian mother in this example employs a directive approach. She separates the children and tells that this behaviour is not allowed. She wants the children to learn what are the rules and norms so that they will learn to play together and learn social behaviour. At the same time she wants to teach children to stick up for themselves.

The following passage shows what parents would have done in the conflict described earlier (they were shown the conflict on video) in which Jim was

West Indian mother and her son

playing with a fire-engine and Otto made persistent attempts to have a turn at playing with it himself.

A West Indian mother:

'I would wait until one of them came to me. I wouldn't have given him the fire-engine immediately. I would say to the child: "I know it's your fire-engine, but can he have a turn soon at playing with it?" I'd want them to learn to resolve conflicts for themselves. They also have to learn to stick up for themselves. One of them is, like: No, it's mine and you can't have it. The other has to learn to be patient.'

A Dutch mother:

'If I saw that the child really didn't like it, I would try to mediate. Then I'd try to find a solution with them and if that meant sitting with them, then I'd do that. Why would I do that? I really want them to understand that they can do things differently, that they should learn too that a child who often concedes does not always gives in, and that you then have to go and look for something else. They have to learn that they cannot always boss other children around.'

A Moroccan mother:

'I would say to that little boy: "Can he play with it too?" I have respect for a child who can keep asking so nice and calmly whether he can play too. I sympathize with the child: he follows him round for quite a while without actually becoming violent. And if that little boy can play with him, they can play together. Why would I do that? Because children have to learn to play together.'

The West Indian mother in this example would not immediately intervene, but would try to get the children to sort it out themselves. She adopts the mediating approach, by means of which she wants them to learn patience, to learn to wait their turn.
The Dutch mother also uses a mediating approach, addressing herself to both children. She wants to offer them alternatives and she wants them to learn that they sometimes have to put up with negative things (delay their gratification).
The Moroccan mother would talk with the children and she too adopts a mediating approach. For her, the most important lesson is that the children should learn to play together.

We have taken the mothers quoted above as examples from a larger group of mothers who were interviewed. If we take all the mothers interviewed, we see minor differences in what they would do – differences in their pedagogical approach. It turns out that the Moroccan and Dutch mothers differ very little in their reactions (Rourou, Singer, Bekkema & De Haan, 2006). They combine a mediating with a directive approach, while the approach of West Indian mothers is more directive than the others. The aims the mothers have for the children are the following:

• to learn that you should not do some things, to learn norms and values;
• to resolve conflicts themselves, to develop independence;
• to play together, to develop socially, to learn empathy and reconciliation with others; to stand up for themselves, to put up with negative things, to be patient, to wait their turn.

All the mothers in the research sample, with regard to the video-clip showing a child hitting and kicking, emphasize the importance of learning the rules of norms and values. Here, it is the Moroccan mothers who particularly want to promote learning how to resolve problems for themselves. Fostering empathy was mainly mentioned by the Dutch and Moroccan mothers.

For Moroccan mothers, playing together and the feeling of connection with the whole are also important aims. Moroccan children will probably reflect this in their behaviour. We saw in chapter 35 that conflicts among Moroccan children are more quickly over and done with.

Forming images

So, what do these findings show? That the reality is not always what you think it is. Perhaps you have an image of Moroccan mothers as being strictly directive toward their children. Such an image does not correspond with the findings from these interviews. You might expect that the Dutch mothers would be most likely to encourage their children to resolve their conflicts independently, but in fact it is the Moroccan mothers. It is not always as you might think. When it comes to child-rearing by parents of native versus immigrant origin, we often tend to look at differences rather than at similarities. This can lead us to form unbalanced images, generalizations and prejudices. Prejudices are based on generalizations. Whether it's a question of Muslims, asylum-seekers or West Indians, the members of such a group are all lumped together; and then from a single event involving individuals of a certain group, we jump to conclusions about the entire group. A prejudice is a judgement that rests at least partially on a lack of knowledge. A prejudice is already in place before there is any observation or evidence. Prejudices can therefore arise when observation of an individual case is too quickly generalized and when the observation is not separated from interpretations, feelings or judgments (Keulen, 2004).

There are many similarities and more especially differences between *individual* mothers, more than there are between groups of mothers. It is also known from research that there are many differences within groups. For example, Moroccan mothers of the first generation often have a very different pedagogical approach from that of the second generation, just as there are great differences between West Indian mothers of higher or lower levels of education (Pels, Dekovic & Model, 2006). These differences between parents of different educational levels hold for Dutch parents too, but there are also differences between mothers and fathers, for instance.

Pedagogical tips to remember

- Ask parents for information and ask their views of bringing up children. Every parent is different and has his or her own approach. We often assume what the parents thinks or does without ever explicitly asking.

- See the parents as individuals and not as representatives of a group. If you know anything about the pedagogical approach of a Moroccan mother, don't immediately generalize: it can lead to misunderstandings and prejudices.

- Begin by looking at similarities and correspondences between yourself and the parent, similarities of pedagogical aims and approach. The most important similarity is that for both you and the parent the child's welfare is paramount. You then know that you are both working for the same goal, what's best for the child. Once you realize that, you can go on to look for mutual differences, and what you will then often see is that you want to reach the same objective as the parent, only in a different way.

37   Upbringing after migration

'My mother moved from Twente to The Hague just after she married because of my father's work. We're talking about the years 1948 to 1955. She missed her family, especially her sister. There was no telephone and no car, so they wrote to each other every week. As for our upbringing, she had few examples and little social contact. She hadn't yet built up a social network. That developed slowly through my father's work colleagues and via the church.

'I know she found it very difficult bringing us up during those first years. The move from Twente to The Hague had a great deal to do with it.'

How do parents know how they should bring up their children? Where do they get their outlook and their knowledge from? And their examples? Mothers differ in their approach when it comes to conflicts: each has her own frame of reference with child rearing.

Social heritage

In the first place, mothers have the experience of their own parents and their own families to draw on. These play an important role in the forming of their ideas on how to bring up children. When it comes to bringing up your own children, your own parents are a very important frame of reference. The values and norms that were maintained in the family, behaviour that was approved or disapproved of, the identification with father or mother, their character and their style of child-rearing, we carry all this with us in our baggage when we set out to bring up children. It has been shown in research on social inheritance that parents display considerable creativity in translating messages that they received during their own upbringing. Parents who, for example, had wanted to have a good education but were unable to, can pass on this desire to their own children and hope that their children will achieve what they were unable to achieve themselves (Bolt, cited in Keulen, 2004).

The Moroccan, West Indian and Dutch mothers in our research gave their view of how to deal with conflict between children, but they also told of the sources of their pedagogical ideas. A West Indian mother relates how she looked for answers to questions about bringing up children:

'You know, my father once told us: "I shall not always be here for you, and everyone has to learn to take responsibility for themselves, and everyone must speak for themselves." ...I try first to find out for myself. If I really can't get there, then I ring my sister. But, well, she's very busy, so I think to myself: wait, I have to try and find a solution myself. And if I don' t find a solution, then I pray. I ask God for support and to help me find a solution, to protect my children where I can't see any solution myself.'

Beside the influence of her own parents and family, the personal character and attitudes of the individual also play a role. Do you cut yourself off from your past background or do you feel most at home with the values that you learned there? Finally, the influence of the social, cultural and religious environment is important; the family and bringing up of children are embedded in that surrounding world.

Migration

The surroundings change, however, when you move and especially with emigration. Moving from the country to the city, from Twente to The Hague, or from Al Houceima to Amsterdam, the social environment changes. Mostly, one loses the support of grandparents or sisters who were previously taken for granted, moreover this new world is governed by different values and norms. Parents have to look elsewhere for support in bringing up their children. A mother who emigrated to The Netherlands relates her story:

'It's not the same. For instance, there is far greater social control in Curacao. It's much broader. When I was growing up there – you had father, mother, and then you also had grandfather, grandmother, aunts, uncles, you had the whole family, and by 'whole family' I mean everybody, even the neighbours.'

We asked a West Indian mother whether child-rearing values were the same in The Netherlands as in the Antilles:

'No, they couldn't be. We have such different cultures, we come from different worlds. Dutch parents bring their children up very freely. Compared with the way I was brought up. I was brought up freely too, but not so free. You have to keep it in check. I don't like generalizing, but I'd have to say that in general upbringing is much freer here. It's much more structured with us.'

What is the frame of reference for bringing up children under such an enormous change of social and cultural environment? Who do you take as an example, and to whom do you go for advice?

Sticking to their own values

A parent can stick to his or her own social values and norms:

> 'No, they're not the same, because I want to bring Ivaron up with respect and I see that this is lacking in Dutch children. They really can do anything they like. (...) He must not get it into his head that he can hit me or swear at me. I won't accept that; it's not good. I was brought up to recognize that my parents were the grown-ups, and that it was not for me to argue with my parents. The way I was brought up, what they said went! So that's how it should be with me too.'

Opting for new elements

Some parents see that they take over things from their new environment:

> 'People here are feelingless and cold, yet we have learned from them to be more open with our children and to build up a good relationship with our children.'

A parent can deliberately select elements from both the old and new cultures and combine them:

> 'I try to find a middle path. I use a few things from my own upbringing and also things from the Dutch that I think are good. My mother would smack me, but she never explained why she did it. Dutch parents, they just talk, always talk and I don't think that's so good either: now and again children need to be smacked! But you have to tell a child why you do it and I didn't have that in my upbringing. I think that's what you have to do, so I have combined the two ways of bringing up children.'

The consequences of emigration have a huge influence on the way children are brought up. Keulen and her colleagues (2004) identify all the changes that have a bearing on this:

Welkom, bienvenue, Murkaza Neka

A conversation on a bench

Mothers meet each other

- *cultural baggage* – differences in child-rearing customs between the new environment and the land or region of origin can make parents anxious and uncertain. Parents deal in different ways with their cultural baggage: some hold fast to customs they bring with them; others (unconsciously) take over new elements; others choose deliberately a mix of elements from their old and their new worlds:
- *differences in communication* – clashes can arise when the language and codes of communication at home and in the outside world are very different. Children in the main learn the new language faster than their parents.
- *social-economic situation* – limited financial resources have an influence on the way children are brought up.
- *altered roles* – such as, for instance, male/female relationships, which are different in the new country; or young families where one partner grew up in The Netherlands and the other in, say, Morocco or Turkey; or children who master the new language more quickly than their parents and have to act as interpreters in matters that are beyond their responsibility.
- *social network* – the circle of family and friends disappears after emigration and the support in bringing up their children that they had from their social network disappears with it.
- *enduring process of migration* – for first generation immigrants, the land of their origin remains their most important frame of reference in bringing up their children. The second generation are pioneers in child-rearing with both old and new values.

Pedagogical points of orientation

- Try to think of the social heritage you can recognize in your own parents or in yourself as a parent. How is this heritage translated into your present situation? (Think, for example, of the importance of education and degrees etc., the legacy of religion, and of the value of material well-being.)

- Do you have (distant) family relatives who emigrated? Do you know what their reasons were for emigrating? How the first generation found the beginning period and how they maintained contact with their country of origin? Do you know how the second generation felt about their background origins?

In conclusion

Gifts and challenges

It's amazing how much two- and three-year-olds can already do! Using 96 hour video-recordings in child day-care centres and play groups we have been able to take a good look at how these two- and three-year-olds deal with each other. We have been able to see how they get along together, how they clash, have their minor conflicts, and how they then once again get along together. We have been able to study the video-images again, we have been able to stop and look at stills, as can be seen by the photographs in this book. We were fascinated: Gianni's sly glance as he secreted from the teacher's gaze a block that he had just taken from Branco, the expression on Vivianne's face when she knows she has been caught throwing sand in the sand-pit, Jeroen's gaze, taking it all in, when Jan and Onno get into a wrestling match over a watering can, the wealth of different approaches Otto can deploy to persuade Jim to let go of his fire-engine, Richella's adroitness in converting her straightforward theft of a plastic orange into a game, and the discipline of Charilain, Raishreri and Nora in waiting their turn to do the ironing, always waiting patiently till the other had finished….

But we also saw how hard Bill cried when his mother left, how Samuel time and again landed up in minor conflict with other children, and how Tayrell and Jerzy tormented Nora. We saw how Bridget submissively endured Anissa's hairdressing treatment and did nothing to stop it, and how the impulsive Wim was simply unable to wait until a toy became free for him. We saw how important teachers are, both in preventing conflicts and in helping children when they couldn't resolve a conflict themselves: teachers who give children confidence, by protecting them when they feel insecure, by their authoritative presence and by giving them a firm footing with rules and routines, by mediating when children had difficulty in getting on together.

Pleasure, curiosity and learning

Being a teacher is no easy work. We have given a glimpse of the multiple aspects that have to be seen to in order to make children confident in a new environment with a large group of other children, to organize the space properly, to play with the children, set rules, make a schedule for activities and create a culture of routines. It is not easy, but it can be learned.

One of the most important conditions for this is that the teacher takes pleasure in children and is able to laugh with them because she can recognise

181

their very special view of life, that she has an inquiring mind for the intense way that children set about discovering life, and that she is able to look with children, in their pleasure and openness, at everything there is to learn.

Another important condition is that she wants to learn and take the opportunities to do so. You learn when you are able to look at your own actions and at the other teachers, but that is not always so simple. Fourteen children in a group often keep teachers so busy that doing and observing simultaneously is difficult. Not only that, there are so many things happening at once – what do you look at? How can you discuss a practice - where so much is happening at the same time – in such a way that you learn from it? Where do you find the time and the energy?

Tools

What we hoped to achieve by writing this book was to make tools available, by providing insight into:
- the connection between 'being together', conflict, conciliation and the learning of social skills and rules;
- the importance of reciprocity in contacts between teacher and child and between the children themselves;
- the distinction between different kinds of clashes, in which different rules are always involved, such as 'keep-away-from-me ' clashes, clashes over objects, I-want-to-join-in-too fusses and clashes over ideas about play;
- the great importance not only of understanding each other, but also of understanding your own feelings and controlling your own behaviour; the distinction between kinds of talking, such as play-talking, doing-talking and think-talking;
- the distinction between the various roles of the teacher - protector, authority and mediator; insight into the different ways of exercising influence: both indirectly – through the organization of the space, structure and ambience – and directly – through contact with individual children, groups of children and the entire group;
- the suggestions for observation and the pedagogical points to remember
- the terms that can orient and guide your attention: cuddle-teachers, eye-and-talk-contact-teachers, the taking-it-in gaze, the questioning look, part-together-part-alone play, and so on.

This book is no textbook. It's a book to discuss, a book of ideas with viewpoints intended to provoke further thought, and a book containing practical tips. We hope that our book will find a way to the kitchen table, because that's where pedagogical change and innovation often starts in children's centres: in the kitchen where teachers talk together and relieve their feelings, where ideas are ventilated. We also hope that a copy might find its way to the board of managers' table, and to the parents' association, and that it will be used for further work on the institution's pedagogical policy for children's social development. It's a book which, we hope, ought to provoke the organization to create room for discussion and learning, and teachers together to create a culture and practice of reflection.

Step by step

In all institutions, we have been able to see how teachers have shaped their pedagogical practice by taking thought about the space, the time with fixed routines and special moments, and about the contacts with parents. Often, in the area of social development, much is left unspoken and a great deal left to the insight of the teachers on the job, whoever they happen to be. We have introduced a considerable amount of material for discussion in this book, too much to be assimilated in one go. By dividing the book into sections and short chapters we have tried to organize the huge field of children's social development to make it rather more convenient of access. Perhaps this may lead to further insight into how to give shape to innovative ideas - a small innovation each time, constantly new insight into one or other aspect - and in the long term to develop one's own overview, to make one's own policy.

Professional pride

Day-care teaching is a relatively new profession. To the general public it would seem obvious that anyone who loves children can do it. Yet at the same time, and particularly in view of our changing society with its attendant rise of tensions and insecurities, it becomes ever clearer just how important it is that children are given the attention that they need. We increasingly realize just how important it is in our society to create a sense of 'togetherness'. The basis for this has to be laid at an early age, the age when children are so naturally impressionable and open to 'togetherness'. 'Doing it together' is the axis around which everything in childcare revolves: security, confidence, community and reciprocal respect for the individuality of every child. When teachers manage to achieve this, they can be proud of themselves. We hope that this book may contribute to the professional pride of the teacher.

Literature

Aarts, M. (2000). *Marte Meo: Basic manual.* Kampen: Aarts productions.

Berk, L. E. (1997). *Child development* (4th ed.). Boston: Allyn & Bacon.

Brennan, M. A. (2005). "They just want to be with us." *Young children: Learning to live the culture. A post-Vygotskian analysis of young children's enculturation into childcare settings.* Wellington: University of Wellington. (dissertation).

Butovskaya, M., Verbeek, P., Ljungberg, T. & Lunardini, A. (2000). A multicultural view of peacemaking among young children. In F. Aurelli & F. B. Waal, M. de (Eds.). *Natural conflict resolution* (pp. 243-258). Berkeley: University of California Press.

Clark, A. & Moss, P. (2005). *Spaces to play. More listening to young children using the mosaic approach.* London: National Children's Bureau.

Corsaro, W. (1988). Routines in the peer culture of American and Italian nursery school children. *Sociology of Education*, 67, 1-26.

Corsaro, W. (1997). *The sociology of childhood.* Thousand Oaks: Pine Froge Press.

Dalli, C. (2003). *Learning in the social environment: Cameos from young children's experiences of starting childcare.* Transitions. European Early Childhood Research Monograph. Series No. 1, 87-98.

Doherty-Sneddon, G. (2003). *Children's unspoken language.* London: Jessica Kingsley.

Dittrich, G., Dörfler, M. & Schneider, K. (Hrsg.) (2001). *Konflikte unter Kindern beobachten und verstehen.* München: Deutsches Jugendinstitut.

Dunn, J. (1988). *The beginnings of social understanding.* Oxford: Blackwell.

Emde, R. N. van, Biringer, Z., Clyman, R. B. & Oppenheim, D. (1991). The moral self of infancy: Affective core and procedural knowledge. *Developmental Review*, 11, 251-270.

Fischer, K. W., Shaver, P. R. & Carnochan, P. (1990). How emotions develop and how they organize development. *Cognition and Emotion*, 4, 81-127.

Frijda, N. H. (1986). *The Emotions.* Cambridge: Cambridge University Press.

Graaff, F.de, A. van Keulen (2007). *Partnership between parents and professionals in early childhood eduction and schools.* The Hague: Bernard van Leer Foundation workingpapers (in press)

Haan, D. de & Singer, E. (2001). Young children's language of togetherness. *International Journal of Early Years Education*, 9, 117-124.

Haan, D. de & Singer, E. (2003). "Use your words" – The teacher's role in the transition from nonverbal to verbal strategies of conflict resolution. *Journal of Early Childhood Research*, 1, 95-109.

Hännikäinen, M. (1997). Beginnings of joint role play in the day-care centre. An activity-theoretical viewpoint. *Acta Psychologica*, 20, 145-153.

Hännikäinen, M. (1999). Togetherness. A manifestation of day-care life. *Early Child Development and Care*, 151, 19-28.

Harper, L. V., McCluskey, K. S. (2003). Teacher-child and child-child interactions in inclusive preschool settings: Do adults inhibit peer interactions? *Early Childhood Research Quarterly*, 18, 163-184.

Hoogdalem, A., Singer, E., Streck, L. & Bekkema, N. (submitted). *Third party intervention in conflicts between 2-4 year old children. A study in Dutch day-care centers.* Utrecht: Universiteit Utrecht.

Jones, E. & Reynolds, G. (1992). *The play's the thing. Teachers' roles in children's pretend play.* New York: Teachers College Press.

Jordan, E., Cowan, A. & Roberts, J. (1995). Knowing the rules: Discursive strategies in young children's power struggles. *Early Childhood Research Quarterly* 10, 339-358.

Keulen, A. van (2004). *Young children aren't biased, are they?! How to handle diversity in early childhood education and school.* Amsterdam: SWP.

Keulen, A. van (ed.) (2004). *Diversity and Equity in Early Childhood Training in Europe. Examples of training practices in the DECET network.* DECET network www.decet.org

Killen, M. & Nucci, L. P. (1995). Morality, autonomy, and social conflict. In M. Killen & D. Hart (Eds.), *Morality in everyday life. Developmental perspectives* (pp. 52-85). Cambridge: Cambridge University Press.

Killen, M. & Waal, F. B. M. de (2000). The evolution and development of morality. In F. Aureli & F. B. M. de Waal (Eds.), *Natural conflict resolution* (pp. 352-372). Berkeley: University of California Press.

Klein, M. D. & Chen, D. (2001). *Working with children from culturally diverse backgrounds.* Albany: Delmar – Thomson learning.

McNaughton, G. (2000). *Rethinking gender in early education.* London / Thousand Oaks: Paul Chapman / Sage.

Ninio, A. & Snow, C.E. (1996). *Pragmatic Development.* Boulder: WestviewPress.

Ogilvy, C.M., Boath, E.H., Cheyne, W.M., Jahoda, J. & Schaffer, H.R. (1992). Staff-child interaction styles in multi-ethnic nursery schools. *British Journal of Developmental Psychology*, 10, 85-97.

Peck, S. (1978). Child-child discourse. In: E. Hatch (Ed.), *Second Language acquisition.* Newbury House, Rowley.

Pels, T. (1991). *Marokkaanse kleuters en hun culturele kapitaal.* [Moroccan preschool children and their cultural capital]. Amsterdam/ Lisse: Swets & Zeitlinger.

Pels, T., Dekovic, M. & Model, S. (2006). *Child rearing in six ethnic families. The multi-cultural Dutch experience.* Ceredigion U.K. / New York U.S.A.: Edwin Mellen Press.

Piaget, J. (1967). *Six psychological studies.* New York: Vintage.

Schaffer, H. R. (Ed.) (1977). *Studies of mother-infant interaction.* London: Academic Press.

Schindler, P. J., Moely, B. E. & Frank, A. L. (1987). Time in day-care and social participation of young children. *Developmental Psychology*, 23, 255-261.

Shantz, C. U. (1987). Conflicts between children. *Child Development* 58, 283-305.

Singer, E. (2002). The logic of young children's (non-verbal) behaviour. *European Early Childhood Education Research Journal*, 10, 55-66.

Singer, E., & Hännikäinen, M. (2002). The teacher's role in territorial conflicts of two and three years old children. *Journal of Research in Childhood Education*, 17, 5-18.

Singer, E., Rourou, A., Bekkema, N., & De Haan, D. (2006). Cultural perspectives on peer conflicts in multicultural Dutch child care centres. *European Early Childhood Education and Research Association Journal* (EECERAJ), 14, 35-55.

Singer, E., & De Haan, D. (2007). Social life of young children. Co-construction of shared meanings and togetherness, humor, and conflicts in child care centers. In B. Spodek & O. N. Saracho (Eds.), *Contemporary Perspectives on Research in*

186

Early Childhood Social learning (pp. 309-332). Charlotte NC: Information Age Publishers.

Singer, E. (2005). The liberation of the child: A recurrent theme in the history of education in western societies. *Early Child Development and Care*, 175, 611- 621.

Stambak, M. & Sinclair, H. (1993). *Pretend play among 3 year olds.* Hillsdale: Erlbaum.

Stern, D. N. (2002). *The first relationship. Infant and mother.* Cambridge: Harvard University Press.

Verba, M. (1994). The beginnings of peer collaboration in peer interaction. *Human Development*, 37, 125-139.

Verbeek, P., Hartup, W. W. & Collins, W. A. (2000). Conflict management in children and adolescents. In F. Aureli & F. B. M. de Waal (Eds.), *Natural conflict resolution* (pp. 34-53). Berkely: University of California Press.

Vygotsky, L. S. (1976). Play and its role in the mental development of the child. In J. S. Bruner, A. Jolly & K. Sylva (Eds.), *Play. Its role in development and evolution* (pp. 537-554). Harmondsworth: Penguin books.

Vygotsky, L. S. (1978). *Mind in society. The development of higher psychological processes.* Cambridge: Harvard University Press.

Waal, F. de (2000). Primates. A natural heritage of conflict resolution. *Science*, 289, 586-590.

Woltering, L. & Tavecchio, L. (2005). Respect voor het verschil. *Pedagogiek in de Praktijk*, 11(24), 12-15.[Respect for gender diversity]

Wong-Fillmore, L. (1979). Individual differences in second language acquisition. In C. J. Fillmore et al. (Eds.), *Individual differences in language ability and behaviour* (pp. 203-228). New York: Academic Press.

Index

About the authors

Dr. Elly Singer (1948) is an educationalist and developmental psychologist. She holds positions as associate professor in Pedagogical Sciences at the University of Amsterdam and in Developmental Psychology at the University of Utrecht. Her doctoral thesis on the history of educational theory relating to young children and childcare gained her international recognition (*Child-Care and the Psychology of Development*). She has conducted research on the quality of childcare, the experience of parents, and has specialized in observational research in childcare centres. In addition, she has done research on the 'inner logic' of schoolchildren: how they deal with foster-parents, with dyslexia or aggression at school. She has published in many practical and scientific journals, including *Human Development* and *Early Child Development and Care*.

Dr. Dorian de Haan (1949) works as a linguist in the Department of Developmental Psychology in the University of Utrecht. In addition to her university lectureship, she is associate professor in Developmentally-oriented education in the School of Education at the INHOLLAND University. She is an expert in the field of children's language development in relation to their environment. Her focus is on the interaction between child and teacher in the multi-ethnic institutions of childcare and primary school. She has published in various journals, including the *Journal of Early Childhood Research* and the *European Early Childhood Education Research Journal.*

Colophon

The social lives of young children
Play, conflict and moral learning in day-care groups

Original Dutch title: *Kijken, kijken, kijken. Over samenspelen, botsen en verzoenen bij jonge kinderen*

Elly Singer
Dorian de Haan
With contributions from Anke van Keulen and Nienke Bekkema

ISBN 978 90 6665 857 8
NUR 854

Translation
Murray Pearson

Cover photograph
Jo Ella Baltus

Cover design
WRIK bno

Layout and typesetting
The DocWorkers

Publisher
Paul Roosenstein

For information on further publications from Uitgeverij SWP:
P.O.Box 257, 1000 AG Amsterdam
Tel.: +31 20 330 72 00
Fax: +31 20 330 80 40
Email: info@mailswp.com
Internet: www.swpbook.com